Understanding the Human Mind

The Power of Healing Thought

Jason Browne

© Copyright 2020 - All rights reserved.

The content contained within this book may not be reproduced, duplicated or transmitted without direct written permission from the author or the publisher.

Under no circumstances will any blame or legal responsibility be held against the publisher, or author, for any damages, reparation, or monetary loss due to the information contained within this book, either directly or indirectly.

Legal Notice:

This book is copyright protected. It is only for personal use. You cannot amend, distribute, sell, use, quote or paraphrase any part, or the content within this book, without the consent of the author or publisher.

Disclaimer Notice:

Please note the information contained within this document is for educational and entertainment purposes only. All effort has been executed to present accurate, up to date, reliable, complete information. No warranties of any kind are declared or implied. Readers acknowledge that the author is not engaged in the rendering of legal, financial, medical or professional advice. The content within this book has been derived from various sources. Please consult a licensed professional before attempting any techniques outlined in this book.

By reading this document, the reader agrees that under no circumstances is the author responsible for any losses, direct or indirect, that are incurred as a result of the use of the information contained within this document, including, but not limited to, errors, omissions, or inaccuracies.

Table of Contents

INTRODUCTION 1

CHAPTER 1: UNDERSTANDING THE MIND-BODY CONNECTION 9

Initial Explorations 9
The Mind-Body Problem 14
   Theories on Emotion 15
   Cognitive Theories 17
   Embodiment Theories 19
The Biopsychosocial Model of Health 21
Clarifying the Language 24

CHAPTER 2: HOW CAN THOUGHTS AND EMOTIONS AFFECT HEALTH? 27

PNI Explained 27
Evidence to Support PNI 33
Understanding Stress 38
Long-Term Reconstruction 42

CHAPTER 3: NEUROPLASTICITY: THE ROAD TO A SELF-HEALING BRAIN 45

Breaking Down the Terminology 45
How the Brain Heals 52
Laughter and Reinvention 57

CHAPTER 4: THE RELAXATION RESPONSE 61

The Founder of Relaxation 61
Learning How to Relax 64
   Meditation 65
   Yoga 69
   Breathing Techniques 72

Meditation Guidance *74*
Simple Techniques *76*
Visualization *77*
Physical Techniques *79*

CHAPTER 5: PLACEBO AND NOCEBO EFFECT: WHEN NEGATIVE THINKING AFFECTS YOUR HEALTH 83

THE PLACEBO PARADOX 84
Placebo Studies *89*
THE NOCEBO PARADOX 91
Nocebo Studies *93*

CHAPTER 6: A THEORY OF CHALLENGE AND THREAT 99

THE TRUTH ABOUT PERCEPTIONS 99
TAKING CONTROL OF YOUR PERCEPTIONS 106
Six-Second Model of EQ *107*

CHAPTER 7: THE PROBLEM OF MIRACULOUS MEDICAL RECOVERIES 113

THE SPONTANEOUS REGRESSION AND REMISSION OF CANCER 114
THE BREDESEN PROTOCOL 123
BOB CAFARO'S INCREDIBLE RECOVERY 127

CONCLUSION 133

REFERENCES 137

Introduction

Doctor John Hagelin once said:

> Happier thoughts lead to an essentially happier biochemistry. A happier, healthier body. Negative thoughts and stress have been shown to seriously degrade the body and the functioning of the brain, because it's our thoughts and emotions that are continuously reassembling, reorganizing, re-creating our body.

Disease and poor health don't inflict the old alone anymore. Generation X is not old in any sense of the word, but they're suffering from chronic conditions that impact their daily lives. More and more millennials are also suffering, which is a thorn in the side, considering how young this generation is in terms of years.

Age is no longer a factor for chronic and debilitating conditions, ranging from diabetes to heart disease. Autoimmune disorders are plaguing the world, and so are inflammatory conditions. It was unheard of for a 35-year-old to have arthritis in their hands, but it's just another day in a doctor's practice today.

Autoimmune disorders prevent us from being as active and happy as we deserve. They strip us of motion, flexibility, and adventure. It gets worse because young people are suffering from heart disease, causing them to miss out on life. It doesn't help that the medical world incites fear surrounding your condition.

Let's not mention the candy-case of medication you're on before you even hit the swinging sixties. Why are you not healthy in the prime years of your life? For what reason must you consider every experience in life from a health perspective before you can enjoy it? Your health is what stands between you and the best life you can live.

However, there's nothing like a little heaving and breathlessness to make you reconsider your plans. Visiting doctors is becoming more painful than the physical pain you suffer from daily, and your mental state is no better. You're tired of aches and pains, and you're sick of being ill. Moreover, conventional medicine is only making you feel worse.

You're familiar with the mind-body connection to some point, but you still have some doubts. The mind-body connection is commonly mentioned in holistic and alternative medicine, and it focuses on the way your mind, body, brain, and spirit act as one being. They influence each other, and there are talks about self-healing.

Conventional medicine has always provided tons of evidence for this and that; however, you're also curious to learn about the other side of this spectrum. Does holistic medicine have a point? Is there a connection between your mind and body that controls every aspect of your health?

There's all this talk about meditation, mindfulness, and yoga, but is there any evidence to support any of these claims? Harvard Health Publishing (2014), which relies on facts and science to support lifestyle choices, confirms that meditation and mindfulness offer extensive benefits to your health through the mind-body connection.

The mind-body connection isn't simply a theory anymore. There's a growing body of evidence to support that holistic techniques can promote the connection between the mind and body to heal the whole system and not just the brain or your condition alone.

A study published in *Social Work and Healthcare* confirms that certain alternative techniques such as yoga and mindfulness can activate specific immune functions to assist your healing journey (Littrell, 2008). Understandably, it's hard to believe in something that hasn't been proved empirically, but the mind-body connection isn't unproven.

It's becoming widely known that our thoughts, emotions, beliefs, behaviors, habits, and mindsets are connected to the way we feel, and ultimately, our health. Thoughts can promote better health, but they can also do harm on a cellular level once you dive into the science behind thinking.

Thoughts are powerful enough to heal the body, and understanding the biological and chemical processes behind each blitz of electricity is essential to using your mindset to change your future well-being. This book covers the science of thinking comprehensively enough for new and seasoned millennials to benefit from the knowledge within.

There's one part of the human drive that never grows old. It's our ability to desire more information and techniques to achieve better potential in our lives. Our passion never fades, even when it's shaken by terrible news and chronic diagnoses. We keep moving forward because it's our primal instinct to persevere at any cost.

Oddly enough, the science behind the mind-body connection and how thought patterns influence it isn't as complicated or technical as you'd expect. Whatever your health conditions are, you can change your direction so your symptoms are relieved, and in some cases, chronic conditions can be reversed with alternative tactics.

There are no miracles or fake promises in science. It's all facts and studies that enhance your ability to open new doors and heal yourself. You don't have to omit your conventional treatments unless you want to. However, using the mind-body connection to heal every aspect of your health is easily achieved with simple strategies.

This book is designed so you can understand how the mind and body are connected, and how this connection affects our emotions and overall well-being. If only you knew sooner that emotions can affect your health on levels never imagined. You'll learn exactly how this happens to ensure you don't allow emotions to overwhelm you again.

Stress and anxiety are two of the worst contributing factors to poor health, whether it's mentally, physically, or neurologically. The evidence will prove that it's possible to think yourself into better health with healing thoughts. The change is simpler than you think, and doubts will be eliminated by facts.

You'll learn about neuroplasticity, neurogenesis, the difference between them, and how you can activate each for optimal brain health, which leads to peak physical and mental health. Neuroplasticity is one of the most misunderstood concepts, but it's a precise process you activate at your whim with practice.

You'll learn about the placebo effect researchers use to trick us into better health, and how you can use it to your advantage. All in all, it comes down to an evidenced field of study called psychoneuroimmunology, which allows you to cultivate extraordinary and natural human capabilities. This field also helps us understand stress in new ways.

Even better, the relaxation response is another biological ability we possess, and it can be triggered by exciting and simple activities. You'll also learn about how it works on a physiological level because it can influence every part of your mind-body connection, including your health.

It's not to be confused with mindfulness meditation because they have varied effects on the body, both of which are incredibly conducive to better health. You'll also learn about the miracles taking the world by storm, and how they work. Are they really miracles, or are they byproducts of the masterful self-healing brain?

It's best to know what the biological factors are behind spontaneous remissions, reversed degeneration, and seemingly impossible cures from conditions like multiple sclerosis. The self-healing brain is within your grasp when you understand how it works, and thoughts are only one aspect of a huge picture.

I've spent a good couple of years researching the human mind and its working process. I've published numerous books focused on understanding the human mind, and my travels and research have opened opportunities that couldn't be achieved before. My writing career, combined with my passion, has also exposed me to the secrets of unlocking the mind.

Researching different cultures, analyzing human thought and behavior, and studying people's character gave me the insight to exploit the connection between the mind and body. There's so much considered as unknown, but the evidence I collected provides definitive answers. My empathetic personality compels me to share my insight and knowledge.

One thing that always strikes the truth is that we can't thrive alone. We need community success to achieve greater meaning and positive changes. My research allowed me to be as healthy as I desire, and my passion is to share this with you so you can join me in a life of indescribable well-being on every level.

Decide whether you're tired of being unwell. Consider what better health would mean to you, and continue reading if you're in this for optimal health, irrespective of your current condition or state.

Chapter 1:

Understanding the Mind-Body Connection

Everyone speaks about the mind-body connection, but what is it precisely? Many people understand that the mind and body are connected. Modern medicine mistakenly treats them as separate entities even though their influence on each other is undeniable, and thus, they should be treated singularly. Your understanding begins by learning how to define this connection, which includes credible research and theories to explain the nature of this connected relationship.

Initial Explorations

There's vast evidence in your daily life that conventional medical practitioners fail to treat the connection and rather choose to treat one or the other in a mind versus body fashion. For example, a physician prescribes medication to treat a headache. They consider what caused the headache on a physical level. Unfortunately, doctors most commonly won't take the next step if there's no apparent cause for your headache, such as trauma. They don't explore beyond the physical aspects of your symptoms. Even if the migraine is a symptom of malignant changes in the brain, such as cancerous growths, conventional medicine only determines that it happened. They'll focus on the biochemical factors that caused the changes in your brain, ignoring possible psychological factors that triggered it.

It works the same from the psychological aspect. Many psychologists, especially the traditional kind who don't practice positive psychology, focus mainly on the mental aspect of your problem. Perhaps you're suffering from depression, and your psychologist might prescribe medication that resets the biochemical factor, but they don't always look at what caused the reaction in the brain. The cause of biochemical reactions in the brain is psychological, and it triggers physiological changes. Many therapists are aware of the mind-body connection, but some simply medicate you. A therapist who understands this connection will also work with you to change psychological factors, and you might not even need medication.

Even though contemporary medicine still functions this way on the physical front, there's a growing body of research that's providing incredible evidence of the connection between the mind and body. Moreover, this idea is in no way novel. It's been explored by philosophers for centuries, which led to scientific research to learn more about it. The debate between what is now known as dualism and monism started long before these theories were designed. Dualism defines humans as mind and body, physical and mental, cognitive and behavioral, or a division between thoughts and actions. This argument is notably traced back to Plato in Ancient Greece, and it has snowballed into a field of theology, philosophy, and science since then (Berecz, 1976).

Plato conceptualized humans as divided beings, even though these entities influenced each other. The mind can influence the body, and the body influences the mind. It's this concept that inspired the psychosomatic medicine approach, which focuses on the psychology of the mind and the 'soma' of the physical being by acknowledging their influence on each other. Theology quickly turned their theory into a trichotomy, which means that they split human beings into body, mind, and spirit. However, there are some flaws with this design, whether you're religious or not.

Christians believe that the spirit belongs to God, and it will leave the body behind when it returns to Him. This indicates a definite division of the three parts. To understand the paradox with this theological view, you need to know about a famous Bible verse. In Matthew 5:28, it's written: "I guarantee that whoever looks with lust at a woman has already committed adultery in his heart." This blows theology out of proportion because it's believed that a thought or imagined feeling is already an action. You think lustfully about her, so you've already behaved wrongly. Theology has many contradictions, but this is the most common one between dualism and monism. day, theology teaches you to live by monism. What you think and the way you behave will either be rewarded or not.

Nevertheless, Aristotle didn't agree with Plato's theory. Monism rejects division, and it acknowledges that every organism in life is unified with great complexity and endless functionality. The body and mind don't simply interact with each other. Every action within the body creates a reaction throughout the entire system. Every part of a human being plays a role in external and internal experiences, and not in such a way that confirms dualistic views where the brain influences the body. The one cannot function without the other is what monism teaches. Think about a flash of lightning. Do you describe the flash as an electrical discharge or a flash of light? The right answer is neither but both. Without light, there's no discharge, and without discharge, there's no light, kind of like the chicken and the egg paradox.

Understanding dualism and monism evolved into modern science, and the question remained the same. Which one is correct? The biggest challenge to this debate is that human beings are complex on every level. It wasn't until scientific evolution allowed neuroscientists to determine the connection between the mind and body that the complexities decreased. Indeed, there are still many complexities we don't understand, but the mind-body connection is quickly being understood. Imaging devices give us the upper hand. In Aristotle and Plato's time, there was too much mystery about what happens within the body when we process thought as one example. Now, we can conveniently watch the electrical pulses surge through the brain on a monitor as we think and feel.

And just like that, the problem was better understood. It vastly depends on the perception of someone when you ask them to explain what they see. Hence, it's a matter of language that makes theology, science, and philosophy disagree. Let's say a young man is giving a speech on stage. You have a theologian, linguist, and neuroscientist in the audience, and they need to explain how the person functions while they're speaking. How does the person function while the words leave their mouths? The scientist records electrical activity in the prefrontal cortex with an imaging device, the theologian says that the person is inspired by their moral compass and divine inspiration, and the linguist will measure patterns in the speaker's words to understand their emotions during the speech.

The three audience members are seeing the same experience, but they're explaining and understanding it differently. It doesn't mean that any of them are right or wrong, although they're all wrong if they use explanations that divide the person's being, body, and mind. The speaker must use their mind to think, and their body reacts to their thoughts physically. You can't take away thoughts because the person would stand there like a mummy. You can't take away physical reactions because their mouth wouldn't move. But together, the mind and body work to create a speech, both physical and mental. One cannot exist without the other, and it's normally a matter of explanation that divides them.

The neuroscientist will say that the prefrontal cortex lit up after a thought popped into the speaker's mind. The brain can't light up without thought, and thoughts can't exist without a brain. Sometimes, scientists don't intend to use dualism in their language. Other times, some people believe that the mind and body are individual entities. The advantage of these seemingly different views is that one thing is agreed upon. Human beings are complex, and so is every inch of their beings. It all depends on how you choose to analyze your body and mind, which is a complete system that can't function if any part of it was missing. Therefore, there can be no division. Monism or the unified theory is correct because we can't break our particles apart without losing our functionality.

The mind-body connection isn't about the mind influencing the body and vice versa. It's about a single organism where even various parts play their roles. You are a single organism, and that includes everything inside of you. You can explain what makes a person a human being from a scientific or theological view, but neither one is more real than the other one. Humans consist of every aspect designed to work uniformly. Behavior isn't more real than thoughts, because the mind-body connection requires the latter to instigate the former.

The Mind-Body Problem

Monism also comes under scrutiny because there are a few misunderstood problems with this idea. Suddenly, it was called the mind-body problem because the connection was doubted once again when other research brought questions to light. Scientists researched various aspects of the 'problem' to understand whether the connection exists and how we can influence the entire network at once. Further theories were developed.

Theories on Emotion

Emotions must be the most complex part of human nature we need to understand. It began when the cognitive appraisal theory was developed by Magda Arnold and Richard Lazarus in the 1940s (Ramirez, 2020). This emotional theory suggests that people evaluate an event cognitively, which depends on the consequence either being pleasant or unpleasant. Maybe you fear calling your doctor because he might have bad news. Your fear is the emotion triggered by the event, which comes before, during, or after it happens. The call is the event, and the consequences can either be the doctor sharing bad news or good news.

Emotions can create a need for a response, and they can be the consequence of a response if you called without thinking about it. The emotion that comes after the call could be negative, such as anger, depression, or fear, or it could be positive, such as relief, gratitude, or happiness. Negative emotions instigate more notable physiological reactions in the body and brain. Therefore, it was the center stage of research in the 1990s. It's not only the negative consequential emotions that spark notable physiological changes. It's also the anticipation of it, which makes us choose to avoid the event because our perception of the risk of negative consequences prevents us from reacting positively. Avoidance isn't a positive reaction.

The reason why positive emotions weren't researched as much is that it didn't react as notably as negative emotions. The majority of psychology and science wanted to focus on how we can decrease the negative responses in the body, but Professor Barbara Frederickson from the University of North Carolina wanted to understand how the positive reactions are so easily dismissed (Lino, 2019). Frederickson knew that multiple components reacted to an emotional event in a short time, and she knew that psychology tended to focus on problems rather than solutions. Positive emotions have fewer autonomic responses in your system, and they can even be harder to recall because of their subtlety.

Positive emotions are closely connected to the subjective well-being, so Frederickson wanted to know why they weren't as noticeable. Would we not have evolved out of positive emotions if they made such a little impact on our lives? The broaden-and-build theory was finally developed in 1998, which includes positive emotions in the research behind the mind-body connection. Negative emotions ignite reactions quickly because of the momentary thought-action repertoire. It happens faster than you comprehend. Simply, negative emotions activate the stress response on a physiological level because the body must be preserved against a threat. That's why fear strikes a more notable physical effect.

This fight or flight response might be physical, but the thought starts in the mind, and the brain immediately releases chemicals that prepare the body for threats. Positive emotions don't have such memorable responses such as running from a bear in the woods. Technically, they don't serve our evolutionary needs in that sense. We can't research positive emotions the same way we do with negative ones. Positive emotions also trigger the momentary thought-action repertoire, except they don't need an immediate response. There's no danger, so you don't enter the fight or flight mode. Instead, the broaden-and-build theory focuses on the broader part of the response.

Given more time, our options to respond automatically broaden, giving us a wider perspective to see the problem or event from various angles. The 'build' part of this theory happens when we choose a positive response, such as finding a creative or unpredictable solution to the problem. You have more time to consider other options, which can help you strengthen social, psychological, and intellectual skills if you consciously use this theory to process information, especially emotions, before taking action. However, the point is that both theories clarify why the mind-body connection is scrutinized from an emotional perspective. Just because you don't always notice the positive reactions, doesn't mean they're not happening.

Cognitive Theories

Cognitive theories confirm that the body and mind are connected, but they emphasize the mental part of the relationship. That's why there's little to no focus on the body in psychotherapy. The psychopathology theory was developed in the 1960s, which focuses on the influence our mind has over the body when it comes to negative emotions. Psychology focuses on the presence that exists between the mind and body, which is often called the mind, mental state, or cognitions. Correcting this mental plain should fix the body and mind because of the connection. A review published in *The Frontiers in Psychology* confirmed that psychotherapy relies heavily on the dualism theory, but it has a good point about the mind (Leitan and Murray, 2014).

Indeed, negative cognitions stir troublesome behavior and physical symptoms, and psychotherapy targets this part of your whole being to improve your reactions. Some psychotherapy approaches target the mind-body monism according to the review, but most of it leans heavily on dualistic views that target the mind alone. However, the review also concluded that psychopathology includes the connection the mind has to the body and brain, even if psychotherapists say they influence each other. It's a matter of explanatory definitions again, but in real terms, this indicates that the connection is considered to some extent, and the mind is confirmed to be grounded in the physical part of your being in this review.

The growth mindset theory is another interesting cognitive approach. Having a growth mindset means you look for opportunities to learn and grow, especially in negative experiences. Adopting this mindset helps you make an effort to improve yourself, and this starts as a thought in the mind-space between the body and brain if you still feel dualistic. The mind can only think in this sense, but it's the connection with the brain that makes the difference. The mind is grounded in the brain, and it can't act on any thoughts without physical changes. The mind and brain work together to send new electrical pulses throughout the brain's network, which is also a physical reaction, and 'physical' is normally defined as the body.

All three 'parts' work together to make changes, which is also known as neuroplasticity. The mind desires improvement, but the brain heightens attention and motivation so the body can carry out the mutual response. Traditional psychotherapy can call it what it likes, but take away the brain's attention and the body won't know what your mind desires. Take away the body, and you'll become a dreamer whose brain and mind want it, but you can't achieve it.

Embodiment Theories

The body completes the unified person, but some theories had to be established to confirm the mind-body connection from the physical aspect. The body affects the mind and brain as well, which proves early cognitive theories wrong. The theory of embodied emotions is the first one. It suggests that our emotions are physical, which, for example, explains the physical reaction you feel when you fear an experience. Chemicals are released in the brain, and your body enters a stress response, but the second part of the theory explains that it's mental as well. Emotions can impact the conscious and subconscious minds, both of which are cognitive beings in psychotherapy. The conscious and subconscious minds can perceive emotions, which is the reason why the physical reaction takes place.

The conscious mind is often called "the thinker." It's where thoughts exist, so when you think something is emotionally painful, the threat reaction starts in the physical body. The second physical theory is called embodied cognition (EC), which lines itself perfectly with the "grounded cognition" found in the psychotherapy review. The mind is embedded in the sensorimotor system in your brain, which is also connected to every nerve cell under your skin. The central nervous system is only part of the nerve map. This explains how sensory stimuli can instigate feelings of pain when you kick your toe against a table. The nerves in your toe are connected to the brain, and the mind is the thinker that perceives the pain or threat.

Embodied cognition explores how the body is part of the perceptual experience and processing of your mind, whether it be the brain or your toes. Your body is actively engaged in the cognitions of what people call the mind, which is grounded in the brain as the conscious and subconscious. Embodiment theories rely on the connection between mind and body when it comes to scientific research and treatment. However, the easiest way you can control the entire network as a whole is through cognitions, which automatically controls the body and brain. The fact that the mind can control all the systems also confirms that it's a single unit.

Controlling the mind or your thoughts are simply easier because they perceptualize everything you experience through sensory stimuli. The human mind is the key to the mind-body connection, which is why psychotherapy targets it and why other forms of psychology have been adopted to focus on various aspects of the connection. Cognitive-behavioral therapy targets the mind, body, and brain; positive psychology uses inspiration from these theories to help people understand how the physical aspect of emotions influences the mind and body simultaneously. Unlocking answers starts in the mind, but there are other factors to consider.

The Biopsychosocial Model of Health

First introduced by psychiatrist George Engel in 1977, the biopsychosocial model of health was the opposition of the conventional biomedical model, which only focused on the physical side (The Mind-Body Connection, 2010). Engel realized there was more to our health, including social, psychological, and biological factors. A holistic approach was needed to treat diseases so it could focus on all aspects. To understand what defines health, we must know what psychobiology, illness, and disease mean. Psychobiology is simply a fancy word for the mind-body connection, but the definition of illness or health differs from person to person. Many people agree that health is the absence of disease; however, is it more than this?

Health is also commonly defined as physical, mental, and social well-being, and this doesn't seem the same as the absence of disease. You might be absent of disease, but your psychological well-being might not be doing so well because you're alone and overworked. You might not even notice it while you keep yourself busy. Maybe you're thriving in your emotional health, but you're struggling to climb the stairs at work without getting breathless. You expect yourself to be as fit as the colleague who races past you every morning, so you consider yourself unhealthy, forgetting that your level of fitness is due to your efforts and needs. That colleague runs marathons every month, so could you rightfully compare yourself to them?

This is how psychosocial factors creep up on you. You can be without disease, but your mental well-being is affected by your idea of what's normal. You think it's normal to see people sprint up 10 flights of stairs. You think it's normal to be overworked and lonely. However, this makes you wonder what normal is. Perceptions of normality often depend on age, culture, gender, and social status, and any thought that you're not normal can impact your unified well-being, such as experiencing physical, emotional, and mental health disruptions. This becomes a problem because many people will be abnormal when they're compared to other genders and cultures as one example.

Even your physical symptoms, such as raised glucose levels, might fall outside of the normal, but that doesn't necessarily make you unhealthy. It's your mental perception of how healthy you are compared to the norms that constitute your physiological response. Are your symptoms so far from normal that it causes you distress? The stair-climber would be distressed if she was once able to sprint up the stairs herself, but there's no sign of ill-health if she was never able to do this. She can cognitively desire this fitness, but she'd have to make physical changes. Her normal isn't the same as someone who trains for monthly marathons. Health is merely an evaluation of how you adhere to the norms of social, physical, and mental factors.

Illness is considered a deviation from the normal, and disease is an explanation that helps you understand the collection of symptoms you experience from this perceived abnormality. Health is a positive ability to function in your daily life, according to your normal. Being unhealthy is a negative state, which must be overcome or treated. The introduction of the biopsychosocial model of health has led to the research and development of new treatment fields, which include the interdisciplinary field of behavioral and psychosomatic medicine and the holistic discipline of health psychology.

The focus of these theories and many others is the human mind because changing your mind will automatically change your behaviors and emotions. Everything physical and neurological will follow the mental shift. So, when will well-being be a complete and simple definition? The answer is when it considers mind and body equally, albeit it will target the mind to ignite automatic reactions throughout the body, which happens thanks to the connection.

Clarifying the Language

It helps to know the difference in the language science uses to determine certain aspects of your mind-body connection, so what is the mind exactly? Is it the same as the brain? The brain is considered a physical part of a person. It's made of countless neurons, blood vessels, and nerves. It also has a specific shape and color, and you can touch it. It's the part of your being that coordinates movements, various body functions, and emotions. A review published in *The United States National Library of Medicine* looks at various parts of the brain, and what functions it controls (Pandya, 2011). The contralateral cortex is responsible for limb movements, emotional reactions are ignited in the amygdala, and speech is controlled by the Broca's area.

However, what the review couldn't establish is the definite location of the mind, even though it was likely allocated to the brainstem because this region is so delicate that irreversible injuries could cause absolute brain death. How could the mind be allocated to one region if thoughts cause physical reactions? It doesn't make sense. The network connects every region in the brain, but it's all physical. The mind can activate any part of the brain or body, indicating that it doesn't exist in a specific space. The physical activation of the brain is undeniably the key to neuroscientists understanding the network, but it's merely the physical part. The mind is not physical. It's a mental existence within the unified body, and it has no tangible cells you can touch.

The mind refers to our consciousness, understanding, and thoughts in scientific terms. The processes also happen on two levels, both intangible. The conscious mind processes thoughts you're aware of, and you know they're happening. The subconscious mind is an automatic processor you aren't aware of. For example, you're subconsciously processing information to think quickly when you need to decide to stop or run a red light. Automatically, the subconscious mind quickly takes over to make you stop. Well, in most cases. The brain and mind are words that define different functions of your whole being. It doesn't mean they're separate entities.

It simply means we talk about them differently because it helps us understand the difference between thoughts and emotions when we use the mind-body connection to improve our lives and health. In simple terms, the brain is a physical thing you can touch, and the mind is an activity of the brain, which can't be touched.

Chapter 2:

How Can Thoughts and Emotions Affect Health?

You've learned about the challenge to establish a solid definition of the mind-body connection. It's time to explore the evidence that supports its existence. More specifically, the existence of the connection between your neural network, mind, and health. The study of this connection is called psychoneuroimmunology (PNI), which is the link between our emotions, thoughts, and the immune system. Certain emotions have the most devastating effects on your whole body. Awareness of what's happening can change your life.

PNI Explained

Psychoneuroimmunology is a long word to remember, but use emotions, the brain, and the immune system to remember it. The biopsychosocial model of health inspired PNI to understand how the connection between the immune system, our thoughts and emotions, and our well-being can become faulty, leading to ill-health. The founder of the biopsychosocial model you learned about in the previous chapter, namely Engel, explains that every cell can be influenced by its environment (The Mind-Body Connection, 2010). Every organ and tissue in your body are your components, and you are a component of your environment, such as society, family, and friends. As such, your experiences and behaviors are influenced on a cellular level as each component within your body impacts the next, and your whole person is a component inflicted by your community environment.

The discipline of PNI studies the interactions between these components on a neural and biochemical level. We can't easily measure a thought, and we can't study it, but we can study the consequences of what each thought and emotion do on a biochemical level. Emotions are a hypothetical construct in science, but they allow the development and hypotheses of research required to know how the immune system and central nervous system function as mutual components. This research led to empirical evidence that proves how the mind-body connection impacts your health. PNI focuses on psychosocial factors that impact your components, such as social support, negative affect, optimism, stress reactivity, and coping mechanisms. It also focuses on biological factors, such as gender, ethnicity, age, genetics, injury, and exposure to harmful components.

PNI also includes the research and development of health and behavioral lifestyles, including sleep, exercise, addictive behaviors, and sexual behaviors. All three areas of research lead to a profound truth about what influences or can be influenced by each one of them. Life stress is the common denominator among the factors, including socioeconomic status, early life experiences, and chronic stress. The research behind PNI leads to further evidence, because certain factors lie within the components of every cell, internal and external. The research to treat the mind-body connection and every component within it has seen substantial strides in improving your vulnerability, resistance, and the onset, progression, and exacerbation of diseases, thus improving your quality of life, physically and mentally.

Whichever component is influencing the next one, it's happening for a reason. The mind-body has a primary directive to preserve you and keep you safe. To expand into the research of how the various components, such as the immune system and central nervous system (CNS), a common goal that could turn into a sabotaged directive, you need to understand the immune system's response and the brain's role in it. The immune system is wonderfully complex. Then again, what isn't complex about the human body? There are two types of immunity, namely innate and adaptive. Innate immunity is the one everyone possesses from birth. The way it works comes back to the cells in the body. Cells, like macrophages and dendritic cells, are part of your body's first-line of defense against threats, injuries, viruses, infections, and anything that changes the quality of your environment.

These cells constantly travel through your bloodstream, looking for abnormal cells or pathogens that indicate a threatening change in the environment with receptors.

If a threat is detected, the cells will begin a cascade of defenses that promote inflammation to keep the area contained so it can recover. Depending on the receptors attached to the immune cell, they'll either bind to the abnormal cell or activate mechanisms to eradicate the abnormalities. Activation makes the cell release proteins called cytokines, which are proinflammatory agents. This is an acute response that either causes inflammation in the area or it can become systematic, causing inflammation throughout the body. Innate immunity isn't specific, and it contains no long-term preservation for you. However, adaptive immunity activates when your innate immunity can't manage.

The adaptive immune response releases a flurry of white blood cells that multiply, and they're called lymphocytes. These white cells contain stored memory of previous threats, and they intend to eradicate the infection or threat with this information. Innate immunity happens in seconds or minutes, whereas adaptive immunity happens over days or weeks. Adaptive immunity relies heavily on macrophage and dendritic cells to help distinguish between normal and abnormal cells in your body. These antigen cells travel back to the lymph nodes, and a release of different cytokines follows. There are varying types of cytokines, of which some are proinflammatory and others are anti-inflammatory. The cytokines that leave the lymph nodes can also produce antibodies, which store information about the current infection.

The adaptive immune response keeps adapting. The memory remains stored in the lymph nodes, and this prevents you from being overwhelmed by the same infection again. Cytokines are the primary driver of inflammation and the communication between two cells, which also makes them neurotransmitters. This means they can carry signals between brain cells, and they promote inflammation, which can even cause cellular changes in your neural network. They can influence and be influenced by other chemicals and hormones in the bloodstream. Countless cytokines have been identified, but PNI focuses on the ones that affect the mind-body connection, especially the cytokines that deploy the biological soldiers that kill threats. Stress hormones can also attract these cytokines out of the bone marrow, the spleen, and lymph nodes.

Chemokines are the cytokines that signal for assistance from every part of your body and brain when a threat is found. The way we understand the cytokine response is that it causes redness, swelling, and pain in the infected area, which tries to cut it off from other regions and heightens your awareness of the injury so you can behave accordingly. This response can also activate the release of C-reactive proteins, which are the ones that push your temperature up and cause rapid heart and breathing rates. This also increases your blood pressure. Even though this is a biological response to make the body uninhabitable for abnormal or infected cells, it's also a negative response if it persists for too long. The neurocognitive response to this change in the body is to adopt "sickness behaviors," including fatigue, pain sensitivity, and social-behavioral withdrawal.

Fatigue intends to help you recover from your ailment, and your pain sensitivity increases so you're aware of further threats from the external environment. The social-behavioral withdrawal occurs because your primal instinct to survive is also a social instinct. You won't intentionally make other people sick. How the immune response communicates with the brain and emotions is through the endocrine system, which is a network of nerves that send signals between various parts of your body and brain. The neuroendocrine system comprises the CNS and the hypothalamus-pituitary-adrenal (HPA) axis.

This is the connection along the endocrine system that connects the hypothalamus and pituitary glands in the midbrain to the adrenal glands throughout the body. It plays a huge role in homeostasis, which is also known as the preservation instinct. Certain macrophage cells are responsible for communicating with the HPA axis when there's a threat in your body, and the HPA axis releases stress hormones through the adrenal glands, called cortisol and adrenaline. The HPA axis is also responsible for signaling the "sickness behaviors." Furthermore, the brain is capable of anticipating threats when you feel stressed, which the immune system doesn't know. The HPA axis determines that you're under threat from external injuries or harm when you feel overwhelmed, and your immune system switches on.

Keep in mind that Engel's theory suggests that every component is affected by another one, which means you can be affected on a psychological level when you perceive threats, whether they're real or not. The conscious mind and your senses are the only things that allow the immune system to know that social threats are near, which makes it respond in anticipation. The HPA axis also releases the most potent anti-inflammatory known as glucocorticoid cortisol, which sadly, remains a stress hormone, meaning that it also promotes inflammation. Cortisol promotes adrenaline, which pumps up the volume of immunity in your body, creating more cytokines and inflammation. Chronic stress responses lead to glucocorticoid sensitivity or resistance, which make cells less receptive to anti-inflammatory agents.

This is where it all goes wrong because the HPA axis is now the cause of chronic inflammation and autoimmune problems where the immune system keeps causing inflammation because there's no natural anti-inflammatory available. The bottom line is that the immune system is our defense against any component that causes harm or a change in the quality of our lives, but sometimes, it can anticipate threats, even if they're not real enough to physically injure us. This anticipation is driven by emotions and thoughts, and your HPA axis can become an enemy that promotes resistance to anti-inflammatory agents found naturally in your body. This conclusion also further proves that your mind and body are connected intricately.

Evidence to Support PNI

The relationship between our brain, emotions, thoughts, and the very mechanism that should biologically protect us from dangers led to numerous studies. *The Journal of Psychopharmacology* published a systematic review to determine the connection between stress, the immune system, and the risk for mental disorders, ranging from depression to anxiety (Calcia et al., 2016). Indeed, psychosocial factors influence our well-being by latching onto the system intended to preserve us. Rejection is painful, which causes negative emotions and stress, and losing a loved one can create the same biochemical effect. It doesn't matter what causes the stress from a social and psychological aspect; the common factor is that it creates a psychological discomfort, which activates the HPA axis and immune system.

This causes macrophages in the brain to work overtime, leading to inflammation and destruction in the hippocampus and other brain regions. The hippocampus is where your amygdala lies, and damage to this gland can cause emotional instability. Damage to the prefrontal cortex can also cause a prolonged absence of conscious logic, which is often required to combat the emotional turmoil you feel. However, the more the emotions and logic in your brain are disconnected, the more the HPA axis continues to respond by activating the immune system and stress hormones, causing even more inflammation. It's a cycle once started. This explains how prolonged stress with no management can cause mental problems and negative changes in the structure of your brain.

Another review published in *The Stress Journal* focused on how we become predisposed to negative patterns that keep this cycle in motion (Deak et al., 2015). Two conclusions stand out. The first is that cytokines interact easier with steroid hormone receptors, such as those found in estrogen, which makes women more prone to the effects stress has on this delicate system. The second conclusion is that our brain's plasticity is more malleable in childhood, resulting in us having more risks of developing the adverse effects of autoimmunity in adulthood if we suffered negative experiences in our younger environment. *The Biol Psychiatry Journal* also published an interesting review (Irwin et al., 2016). focus of this review was to determine if our lifestyles can affect the balance between emotions and the immune system.

Sleep was the main focus because a lack of it can cause a stress response to activate, leading to prolonged issues. Sleep disturbances cause systemic inflammation throughout the brain and body. However, the main question people have is whether prolonged exposure to this effect can also lead to other chronic and life-threatening conditions. A study was conducted by Doctor Gailen Marshall at the University of Mississippi Medical Center to understand whether autoimmunity leads to other conditions (Marshall, 2011). Gailen found an undeniable connection between inflammatory effects and immune dysfunction.

Thoughts and emotions, including stress, must regulate the immune system because of its inability to absorb information from the external world itself, and the immune system becomes automated when there's a lack of proper regulation, leading to a breakdown that causes further susceptibility to illnesses and abnormal cells. Suffering from the common cold becomes more regular, and you can even suffer from the reactivation of previous infections that the immune system already took care of. Stress and inflammation are related enough to make you sick. It can change your quality of life, and it can decline your health. Further investigation has proven the dire consequences of the failure to regulate thoughts and emotions to prevent this autoimmune and inflammatory condition.

The effects can even show externally. Psoriasis is a chronic condition that exposes itself as red and scaly patches on your skin that itch like hell. Little do people know that psoriasis is caused by the speedy and overproduction of skin cells. The human body can excrete excess skin cells when they're no longer needed, which explains dandruff. However, the immune system wrongly activates cytokines to produce the overgrowth of skin cells, which your natural excretion can't handle. Stress also causes this reaction to multiply, and even worse, itching aimlessly and being in pain is a reason to stress, causing the cycle to begin all over again.

Cancer has also been the focus of many studies under PNI because it's the presence of abnormal cells, and *The Journal of Brain, Behavior, and Immunity* reviewed these studies (McDonald et al., 2013). The conclusion confirmed four painful facts. Immune system abnormalities in response to stress were most prevalent in women with the genetic risk factors for various cancers. Furthermore, there's a connection between a lack of social support, depression, women with breast cancer, and immune response activation. Women who suffered from breast, ovarian, and cervical cancer were also showing autoimmune dysfunction after admitting how stressed and lonely they were. The most painful conclusion was that stress was related to lower survival rates among cancer patients.

Cancer is bad enough, and it already removes so much joy from our lives. We don't need to worsen it with stress or negative emotions, such as those related to depression. It's so hard to say you need to manage your stress if you have cancer, but managing it could improve your quality of life and increase your survival chances. That should give you enough motivation to at least consider how stress is worsening the condition that no one deserves in this life. Anyway, autoimmune disorders have also been linked to cardiac problems in another review published by psychiatrist and surgeon Roger Ho and his associates (Ho et al., 2010). The increase in blood pressure and heart rate during this stress-related immune response over prolonged periods wears your arteries down, leading to coronary artery disease (CAD).

The evidence supports the connection of your brain, immune system, and your emotions, while it also confirms how detrimental it can be if left alone. Stress seems to drive many negative emotions and disorders, and it's stimulated by many causes from lifestyle choices to a lack of social support. What this conclusive evidence teaches us is that emotions and thoughts can challenge your health on every level. Stress affects every corner of your being—mental, physical, and emotional.

Understanding Stress

Stress can't only be defined as an emotional reaction once you know the truth. It's defined as any experience that changes your physical, mental, and emotional well-being. It's a response to something that requires attention. Everyone experiences stress daily, but the type of stress and how you respond to it matters. You must start recognizing stress. The symptoms include mood changes, decreased libido, sweaty palms, clammy skin, insomnia, digestive problems, and diarrhea. It also includes dizziness, frequent illnesses, migraines, a lack of energy, and grinding teeth. Don't overlook muscle pain, the tension in various muscle groups, trembling, and a racing heart, either. Psychological signs of stress include difficulty concentrating, memory lapses, and anxiety.

Emotional signs include irritability, anger, and frustration. Physical signs include unintentional weight changes, erratic menstrual cycles, and high blood pressure. Behavioral signs include a loss of interest in self-care, using substances to cope with it, and losing interest in your previous passions. Stress is primarily caused by the fight or flight response, which allows the HPA axis to do its thing. The increased blood flow can stop the oxygen from reaching your muscle groups, which explains the tension. Your digestion and higher cognitive functioning slow down so you can direct your energy to the threat. External factors also constantly influence the stress your body feels, such as smoking and drinking alcohol.

There are four different types of stress. The first one is called acute stress, which is the short-term stress response that doesn't leave lasting effects. It can be driven by positive or negative stress.

Episodic acute stress is the frequent bursts of short-term responses, which can also become problematic if you're using negative stress to motivate yourself at work daily.

Eustress is a positive kind of stress, even if you think it can't exist. It's exciting, fun, and it keeps you energized through controlled surges of adrenaline when you're riding a roller coaster or chasing a goal.

Chronic stress is the worst kind. It's when stress becomes an inescapable, never-ending cycle. It can be the result of an abusive marriage, terrible job, or the struggle to readjust to life after a loved one dies. It also often stems from trauma or childhood instability where the highly-impressionable plasticity has latched on to negative emotions.

Stress might be housed under the umbrella that incorporates the mind-body connection, but it's frequently activated by two main kinds of emotions that influence our thoughts and responses. Keep in mind that thoughts can also stimulate emotions. The positive kind of stress is tied to excitement and happiness, but the negative kind of stress is intertwined with fear. Even small doses of negative stress can motivate us to finish our work before the deadline or to stop at a traffic light. However, excessive amounts of this type of stress only lead to autoimmune and inflammatory responses.

Chronic stress is the main focus of PNI for a reason. It impacts our health, and we must understand what internal and external environmental components make us more likely to experience prolonged negative stress. Having negative stress responses ignited by fear daily is a recipe for health problems. Investigate whether your work, family, or home dynamics are causing fear. Do you feel anxious about your work daily to a point where it affects your functionality? The second reason why fear becomes a reality when we lose our jobs, divorce our spouses, or experience the death of a loved one is uncertainty. This certainly stirs anxiousness, worries, fear, and every other emotion that leads to negative stress. Human beings fear nothing more than sudden and unexpected uncertainty.

Previous trauma is another common reason for suffering from fear. Take someone who was abused by their father as a child. Their fear awakens every time they see anyone or anything that reminds them of this trauma. The same applies to someone who survived a horrible car accident. They might seem to function normally in their daily lives, but they don't even realize the subtle symptoms of negative stress that accompanies them on their drive to work daily. Remember that the mind has two methods of processing information. You have the conscious mind that deliberately pays attention to the changes in your body, and you have the subconscious mind, which is the processing you use when you don't even notice how tense you are in the car until something catches your eye to make you hit the brakes. Anticipatory stress leads to an immune response nonetheless.

One thing you need to realize is that everyone experiences stress differently, too. Don't expect yourself to experience the same physical symptoms and mental decline as your best friend. Moreover, you can experience negative stress in numerous ways, even though you remain the same person. Maybe you're more sensitive to gunshots, but your subtle digestive problems are dismissed when you pursue the latest deadline at work. The magnitude of stress differs, even in a single mind-body connection. Stress is also defined as the perception and evaluation our brain runs through those mental processes, both conscious and subconscious. The brain is a curious organ, and it's always trying to make sense of the environment.

This processing leads to a thought, which creates an emotion, and this is what determines how you respond to the stressor. Emotions can also influence the thought during processing, which happens in the case of trauma survivors. The driver is already fearful at a subconscious level before her mind processes a thought, and her thought only multiplies the emotional response that triggers the defense system. Nevertheless, stress can be perceived, or it can already exist below your awareness. The stimulation for stress can be sorted into three categories—major changes that affect you, major changes that affect the community, and daily struggles. The first category is normally beyond anyone's control unless you think you stop a tornado from tearing through your hometown.

This category is universal, which means it normally affects a group of people. The second category covers stress that is beyond your control, only affecting you, and often has long-term effects. Writing exams and the death of loved ones fall into this category. The final category covers your daily trip to work, workload, and small disagreements with loved ones. The review of cancer patients was disturbing, but negative stress driven by fear has the same effect across the board when it comes to recovery. Increased fear before surgery can increase your recovery time (Newman, 2016). It even increases the time the wound takes to heal. Negative stress and emotions wear an irrefutable nasty mask that only makes healthy people unhealthy.

Long-Term Reconstruction

In case you thought it couldn't get worse, negative stress can reconstruct the brain itself. Neuroplasticity doesn't die of old age when you mature, which means the cycle only becomes more harmful with every fight or flight response triggered by fear or uncertainty. The senses are the eyes to the external environment, and anything you see or perceive as danger will activate the emotional response from the amygdala, causing fear to trigger the HPA axis to respond with a defense strategy. The changes that take place might be long-term, including the constriction of blood vessels in the lungs and heart. However, the brain also undergoes a transformation when this cycle continues to play out.

The CNS consists of the sympathetic (SNS) and parasympathetic nervous systems (PNS), and the latter is responsible for hitting the brakes when the threat is perceived to be less harmful than you first thought. This system can be overworked, causing failure. Moreover, the fight or flight response can activate faster than your conscious mind comprehends. Your body has already tensed before you hit the ground when you trip over something. You didn't even realize you're about to hit the ground before your response activated. The hypothalamus has already sent the corticotropin-releasing hormone to instruct the release of cortisol.

Without regaining control of the parasympathetic nervous system to hit the brakes, you stand a chance of reconstructing the brain. Chronic levels of cortisol don't only damage the neuropeptides in the brain, which design new synapses between brain regions. It also harms the neurotransmitters that travel through them, namely serotonin, which is a mood hormone that's essential to your well-being. Cortisol inhibits it, so your mood changes are physical, too. Serotonin is also a valuable chemical in your circadian rhythm, which is the body clock that regulates your sleep habits. There's nothing that cortisol and inflammation touch that doesn't backfire into a cycle of more stress. The structural changes in the brain lead to burnout and an inability to problem-solve.

How would you solve the problem of your health if you can't use the network designed to do it? Everything you do, the way you think, and the way you feel impact habits in the brain. Cycles become habits, and the synapses that connect one cell to another will be under attack. How often they're under attack is your choice. Controlling the brakes on your mind-body connection is possible, and you'll learn about the positive plasticity in the next chapter.

Chapter 3:

Neuroplasticity: The Road to a Self-Healing Brain

The previous chapter painted a picture of everything we don't want and how the brain can be an enemy; however, this is only half the picture. Neuroplasticity is the key to unlocking positive changes in your well-being. Discover the power that lies within your ability to change the brain, understand how it works, and learn to help the brain heal itself and your body. Neuroplasticity is a skill, advantage, and mastery that can improve your life and well-being.

Breaking Down the Terminology

You've established how the mind and body share a connection through the CNS and immune system and how psychological stress triggers physical responses in the brain. This response travels through the nervous system and into every part of your body, which triggers detrimental changes and disruptions. This simply summarizes what you're learned so far, but it serves a purpose. The common denominator in the mind-body connection is the brain. The crucial lesson being that the brain is plastic, and it can remodel, reorganize, and change its structure and functions, which helps it adapt to the necessary changes better. Neuro is a word used to describe the physical brain, but plasticity is also defined distinctly. Think about how tough a sheet of plastic is.

You can bend, fold, and twist it, but it remains intact. You're an external force molding the sheet. You're giving it a new experience, and what happens when you keep folding the sheet? Plastic is a hard substance, but it's also malleable with effort. A visible fold appears if you persistently fold the same crease in a sheet of plastic, and it eventually keeps its shape. Plasticity is the formal word used to describe any physical substance that has a weak enough construct to be influenced by external forces and experiences. However, the substance must also be strong enough to not mold at once. While everyone has a different explanation of neuroplasticity, it's known as the process in which you change the functions and structures of the brain or the adaptation and regeneration of your brain after trauma.

The most common definition is that the CNS can change structure and functionality with the help of experience. It helps to know the structures within the brain better before understanding how it changes. The brain consists of billions of neurons and nerve cells, smaller than the eye can see. Connecting these neurons are synapses, which you learned about previously, but what makes up our synapses? Synapses are the tissue between neurons, and they're made of three main parts.

There are presynapses and postsynapses, and they're separated by synaptic clefts. A cleft is a space or opening. The presynaptic part is made of many tiny vesicles that contain neurotransmitters, such as dopamine and serotonin.

The postsynaptic part of the synapses also contains a myriad of vesicles, but these are intended to capture neurotransmitters from the presynaptic fibers through the cleft or space. Every receptor inside the postsynaptic vesicles is specifically tuned to accept certain neurotransmitters. A neuron is activated by a stimulating experience, which causes an electrical jolt that instructs the presynaptic and postsynaptic fibers to communicate across specific clefts that connect them to produce a certain response. This is called the action potential that leads to neurotransmission or communication.

Various neurons across the brain can activate together as both synaptic fibers function to achieve certain transmissions. A neuron that receives transmissions must also have the ability to ignite an action potential to communicate with the next neuron. The ability that your neurons possess to ignite and strengthen these communications across the desired network is what we call neuroplasticity. Neurons rely on experience to design new synaptic networks that connect cells that weren't connected before. On the other hand, this communication synapse degrades if it isn't used often enough. The energy of the cell declines, and it can't produce enough electrical discharge for the action potential.

The ability to develop new synapses is the same reason why people recover after brain injuries because, sometimes, it's the functionality that changes, leading to missing or damaged synapses. There's a noticeable difference between how your brain functions and its structure. Functionality refers to the ability neurons possess to communicate across networks, which means the neurotransmitters and synapses are crucial to how the brain works. The brain's function is also physical, but it's an ever-changing system. Every synapse isn't functioning at every moment of the day. Functional changes can include what is called denervation supersensitivity.

Denervation refers to damage, which is brought on by injuries. Supersensitivity is the brain's homeostasis that tries to repair the damage. The brain realizes that the connection between two neurons is lost, and it tries to restore this function so communication can resume. You can call this the brain's self-preservation or defense against damage triggered by physical changes. Keep in mind that stress is also a physical change. Postsynaptic fibers will attempt to repair the lost connection by releasing small amounts of glutamate, which is an excitatory neurotransmitter that intends to excite the action potential again.

This release also increases the positive charge within the neuron attempting to repair the damage. The neuron then expels calcium and magnesium through the postsynaptic fibers to strengthen the synapse that suffered damage. This process is called potentiation, and it consists of three changes to the functionality of your neurons and networks, leading to long-term potential for enhancement or repair. Every neuron becomes more cooperative to produce electrical charges again, and the potential to increase the strength and survival of a specific synapse is boosted.

The third potentiation of this functional part of your brain is that it improves the association between two neurons, leading to the potential for larger networks to improve through collective plasticity. You can also depress the long-term functions in a specific network, much like changing a bad habit, by changing the way the brain functions. Functional changes also come with the advantage of developing structural changes with persistence. The brain will prune, sprout, and strengthen physical connections through experience.

The number, size, and density of synapses increase as you keep practicing new functions by experiencing different events, thoughts, and emotions. The Canadian Center for Behavioral Neuroscience at the University of Lethbridge examined the relationship between the constant development of the brain and the main mechanism of plasticity on a structural level (Kolb et al., 2013). Kolb and his colleagues found that structural plasticity happens with three types of experiences.

Experience-independent plasticity is the first one, which is everything the brain experiences during the prenatal phase of our lives. Our brains first start developing structural connections before we're born, and this is mainly dependent on genetic influence and our mother's lifestyle. Certain neurons will fire together, making you enter this world with skills and talents embedded in your brain already. This means that certain communication networks are stronger and more prominent than others, but it doesn't mean you're naturally capable of playing a musical instrument. The groundwork is laid, but your experience after birth is what makes you master the skill. It's funny how experts once thought that plasticity ended after childhood, but it didn't. It might not happen at the rate it once did, but it still happens.

Nevertheless, the second plasticity that shapes your structure in the brain is called experience-expectant plasticity. This type of experience helps your neurons connect independently without other networks being involved. For example, the retinal ganglion is a network of neurons that collect information through your sight that travels into the brain via the neurons between the eye and brain. The synapses between these neurons work unitedly for both eyes when you're young, but each eye tends to build its own network as you mature. The eyes make a great example because losing your sight in one eye means the other eye can work independently to process information from an experience. Otherwise, you'd lose all image processing if you go blind in one eye.

The third type of restructuring is called experience-dependent plasticity. This is the experience you encounter throughout life by learning and experimenting. Kids use this type of plasticity to develop their skills further on those networks that designed prominent connections through genetically-inherited talents. The brain changes structurally when your experience changes, which can include moving homes, trying to solve a problem, adapting to the changes that come after an injury, and learning new skills. This is the type of experience you can control with new habits, thoughts, emotions, and external experiences.

Plasticity requires one of the three types of experience. You can't simply change the first type, but you have full control over the last type. Restructuring the brain through experience-dependent changes has long-lasting effects. Another self-healing process is called neurogenesis, which is the defense strategy the brain uses to compensate after injuries or the death of neurons. Neuroplasticity can promote neurogenesis, but the latter is a regeneration of cells. Neurons that don't fire or are part of a network will be eliminated naturally from your brain. Neurons technically have a mind of their own, which is called the nucleus membrane. This is the intelligence of every cell in your body, and it's a matter of survival of the fittest between neurons.

Neurons dispel other neurons if they're weakened or damaged, and each one has a shelf-life. Old neurons die, and new ones are born thanks to the brain's desire to preserve itself, and the newer neurons eliminate older neurons that weaken networks (Bergland, 2017). Neuroplasticity can guide the brain to increase regeneration in specific regions, but neurogenesis is the birth of new cells. Neurogenesis also happens when new cells are born to replace neurons that died from injury or degenerative disorders, such as Alzheimer's.

To summarize the terms better, neuroplasticity happens structurally and functionally by improving the layout of your brain and the way it works. This can be achieved by experiencing the right stimuli to promote the structural improvements when the synapses restore or multiply their networks or the functionality when they strengthen these communications. Neurogenesis is a potential byproduct of neuroplasticity that even helps us reverse degeneration and rebuild a network, which was previously injured or dead. Neuroplasticity is the ability you possess on a biological level to intentionally reinvent yourself, which can also lead to improved health once you have those emotions and thoughts under control instead of allowing them to disrupt your immune system.

The intention is the key, even by psychological standards. You won't learn something new if you don't intend to learn. Learning and experiencing are your gateways to neuroplasticity. Every lesson has the potential to lay new networks. Every experience is a possibility. A growth mindset allows you to pursue lessons and experiences that teach the brain new tricks. An enriched environment combined with focused attention, novelty, and a few challenges get your neurons firing. Doing this for one hour a day over five to six weeks makes it possible to design strong networks. It only takes a neuron eight weeks to mature enough to function at its prime (Ackerman, 2018). This opens a whole new can of opportunities for you to use biology and biochemistry as a health hack.

How the Brain Heals

The brain is the center of the mind-body connection, and neuroplasticity allows us to restructure and recondition the brain, which extends to the reconstruction of your body and mind. However, how does this knowledge relate to your health, and how can you use it to improve your health? Let's mention a case study because it was one of many that inspired my research with neuroplasticity. A friend of mine, who we'll call Amy for anonymity purposes, suffered a devastating brain injury a few years back. She was struck by a metal rod against the temporal lobe in an accident. Amy was always well-articulated and intelligent, but it was shocking to see her after the accident.

She obtained a brain injury in the posterior superior region within the temporal lobe, which made it difficult for her to comprehend language and speech. She was unable to speak a full sentence before her words grew longer and slurry. She'd just stop speaking halfway through, and she'd close her eyes while she breathed deeply. Amy opened her eyes to complete her sentence, but it normally changed direction. She would express how she was suddenly exhausted. Amy needed to sleep every two hours during the first few weeks, and speech made her more tired.

It was sad to see a good friend in this condition, but she made great strides within four months. She was speaking again, even though her words were still slower than normal. Amy explained what happened right after her accident. She woke up to a state that trapped her in her mind. Her thoughts were as clear as daylight, but she couldn't articulate her words. Trying to express herself made her feel like she was about to collapse from fatigue. The energy her brain required to compensate for all the damage was too great at this stage. Imagine being trapped in your mind, being unable to communicate. It wasn't only her speech. Amy wasn't able to write at this stage, either. Her thoughts and emotions were bouncing around without an outlet.

The point of this story is that Amy recovered through training her mind immediately. She made an effort to change the plasticity of her brain and create neurogenesis. You'd never think that Amy suffered a traumatic brain injury only five years ago when you speak to her in her renewed articulation and intelligence today. Never underestimate what your brain's healing powers can accomplish. *The Journal of Translational Research in Traumatic Brain Injuries* published evidence that the brain can heal itself after traumatic brain injuries (Su et al., 2016). They established that the brain goes through three changes immediately after an injury, irrespective of how it occurred.

The first change is immediate where neurons begin to die, weakening networks that used to communicate with each other. This only takes a day or two to happen, and the brain might even turn its attention to networks used less in the past to compensate for the dying networks. A newly blind person's other senses heighten within 48 hours of the loss of sight because other networks activate to compensate for the loss in their retinal network.

The second change happens over a few days. The networks within the damaged region will change from inhibitory to excitable, meaning the synapses will try to establish electrical discharge again. The brain doesn't give up immediately, and it works on building new networks in this region. Healing also involves neurogenesis as the brain intends to restore functions to this area.

The third change happens over weeks. The synapses are created, and the network connects new neurons and cells as the brain continues to remodel the damaged region. Old and dead neurons are gone, and the new neurons are maturing. This is the crucial stage where neuroplasticity and brain training have been the most successful in strengthening these networks. Not training them will only let the brain know this region isn't important anymore.

Neuroplasticity has been a phenomenal treatment in people with traumatic brain injuries. The sooner it starts, the better your chances of rebuilding networks that were damaged. The study also suggests that neuroplasticity can slow down the progression of degenerative disorders. Getting lots of sleep also promotes the regeneration of new neurons because your brain has the energy it needs to do this. How you choose to train your brain doesn't matter, but it's most effective in the weeks following an injury. You have to challenge your brain to use this region to promote neurogenesis. Switch off your iPhone, and use an old map to find your destination instead.

Try new things like learning a new language or signing up for courses at a college. Remember that experience enhances neuroplasticity, so provide it. Neuroplasticity also provides other benefits (Ackerman, 2018). It can help stroke patients recover skills by practicing repetition and specific tasks. It can also promote better emotional health to eradicate depression and anxiety, which keeps the immune system from switching over to autoimmunity and chronic inflammation. Even chronic pain can be diminished by rewiring the way your brain functions. Pain is an experience, and you can alter your experience by laying new networks.

One of the main reasons neuroplasticity reduces pain lies within relaxation techniques. Teaching the brain how to relax resets the parasympathetic nervous system to hit the brakes when your immune system is overworking. The secret to help your brain experience what's needed is to challenge it with everything you can. Trick your brain into working different networks by using your left hand if you're right-handed. Start walking up the stairs with your less dominant foot. Keep trying new things, visiting new places, and adapting to new thoughts and feelings. You can influence neuroplasticity internally and externally.

Changing the way you feel is an internal stimulation, and visiting a new city is an external experience. Read a book you've never considered before, or watch a movie that doesn't fall into your preferred genre. Any experience gets the brain to process information, and this helps it to awaken dormant areas. Never forget the connection when you experience life, events, and emotions because the mind, body, and brain need to work together. The body and mind's influence on the brain will cause changes. Everything you feel, think, see, smell, and taste shapes your brain, and so does the way you behave, talk, and interact with other people.

Science found an experience to study neuroplasticity because it offers external and internal changes in your mind-body connection. Understanding the science behind laughter as an experience helps you see how beneficial neuroplasticity is to your health.

Laughter and Reinvention

Laughter, smiling, and humor have been studied extensively to understand how neuroplasticity improves your health. Laughter is an abrupt change to your internal environment, including the body, mind, and brain. It's sudden, sometimes unexpected, and it releases neurotransmitters, such as dopamine, serotonin, and endorphins. It also immediately suppresses cortisol and adrenaline, which quickly changes your mood. A changed mood resonates throughout the mind-body connection because your thoughts and emotions become positively elevated. Laughter is the greatest natural medicine for stress, because it triggers positive consequences more powerful than fear (Scott, 2006).

It also produces antibody cells that promote T cells, which are the specific kind of immune cell that doesn't cause systemic immune responses throughout your body. T cells focus on specific abnormalities, which means that laughter boosts the immune system and prevents autoimmune dysfunctions caused by stress. Laughter even brings a change of perspective when you learn to giggle at a challenge instead of fearing it. The brain translates this information more accurately, preventing it from identifying threats that aren't real.

The immune system gets an overall boost because your lymph nodes also release lymphocytes to reduce pain.

Laughter is contagious enough to help us connect with other people, and being social is required to keep the mind-body connection at peak health. Laughter and smiling are signs of goodwill or intention toward another person. It's a friendly gesture, but laughter trumps smiling because a smile can be faked, but laughter is a far more physical behavior. Your self-esteem and optimism also increase while you're giggling away, which are well-received skills in social groups. These two skills also help you develop better coping mechanisms for negative experiences that stress you, decreasing your depression and anxiety further. It even offers us a distraction from painful or negative emotions that keep the brain focused on bad experiences, such as guilt, anger, and frustration.

The abruptness of laughter has physical benefits, too. It releases tension in your muscles as your energy needs to focus on the workout you're experiencing. Your diaphragm and stomach get a quick workout, which also increases oxygen flow. The energy your diaphragm uses to laugh can even help you lose weight. It burns calories when your muscles are contracting and releasing. Three major health benefits come with a good giggle. It reduces your blood pressure, which has led to the development of laughter yoga. Practitioners simply provoke laughter in a class, and the eye contact between them makes it more real, striking the perfect contagious factor.

The second incredible benefit to your health is when laughter makes you breathe better. Research published in *The Journal of Biological Psychology* identifies how laughter affects the respiratory system (Fry and Rader, 1977). The physiological response to laughter increases your respiration and heart rate similar to physical exercise, which ensures better oxygen consumption and flow. Understandably, it's hard to catch your breath when you're bent over laughing, but pay attention to how much better you breathe after it. Your heart will also thank you for mirthful laughter according to Harvard Medical School (Skerrett, 2010). Laughing improves the way your arteries contract and release, which prevents chronic heart diseases related to your arteries.

There's a lot of evidence that laughter enhances your health on many levels, and it doubles as an experience for the mind, body, and brain. It's a convenient and free stress management tool that offers physical changes, which also happen in the brain. However, laughter must be genuine to achieve this effect. Fake giggles don't offer the same abrupt change in your environment. You need to stimulate genuine outbursts and enjoy them until your stomach hurts. Laughing with friends is easier than doing it alone. Use inspiration from laughter yoga by making eye contact to guarantee that it's contagious. The more you laugh, the more they'll laugh, which makes you laugh even harder. Go to the movies, and watch something that strikes every humor bone in your body.

Planning a game night or party at your place gives you enough control to make sure laughter is on the cards. Boost laughs without the social aspect, too. You can't be with friends and loved ones all day long, so make sure you smile and laugh alone. The first trick is to become aware of your complaining nature if you have one when you get frustrated. Rather find a reason to laugh about your misfortune. This will change your brain's perspective of the situation. We often laugh about things in the future, so imagine that you're explaining to your best friend what happened.

Make it your goal to ignite laughter in your imagined person, and you'll be giggling at the least. It's a matter of faking it until you make it. Indeed, fake laughter doesn't have the same response. However, you might just burst into laughter when you try aimlessly to fake it. Actions lead to reactions, so fake your smiles and laughter until your brain gives up and makes you laugh. Instigating genuine laughter in yourself is also simple thanks to the digital age we live in. Keep your media trigger-happy by joining countless humor groups on social media, and spend time daily watching stupid videos on YouTube. You won't believe the dumb things people try.

Your mind-body connection and the art of neuroplasticity make it possible to improve your health, life, and happiness. Being aware of it and learning a few tricks is a start. However, you need to know how to get the parasympathetic nervous system in full functional glory again so your immune system won't sabotage your health.

Chapter 4:

The Relaxation Response

The relaxation response protects the body and mind connection from stress, illness, and any health problems that come your way. Moreover, it can keep the brain from succumbing to stress when you want to rewire your brain with neuroplasticity. Learning to relax isn't as natural as you assume, especially not if you've been battling stress and inflammatory health conditions for a long time. Whether you want to nip future health concerns in the bud or you want to work toward a self-healing brain that promotes better immunity, some relaxation techniques, such as meditation and yoga among others, are proven to work.

The Founder of Relaxation

Relaxation has been around as long as ancient cultures. It's been there since the beginning of civilization, but it wasn't until the twentieth century that it was brought to light by science. Doctor Herbert Benson from Harvard Medical School and the Herbert Benson Institute for Mind-Body Medicine is a name synonymous with relaxation in modern science (Harvey, 2017). Benson was but a young cardiologist in the 1960s when he was intrigued by transcendental meditation, and he snuck meditators into his laboratory at Harvard to study them under the moonlight. Meditation and relaxation weren't a large part of science at this stage, and studying it could lead to career suicide. Benson was curious about Harvard Physiologist Walter Cannon's work in 1915, which led to what we know as the fight or flight response.

Benson's work began with seasoned meditators by connecting respirators, heart rate monitors, and electrodes to measure the physiological changes in their bodies while they meditated. His studies led to a massive breakthrough in modern medicine, and he recorded a myriad of health changes in these participants. The transcendental meditators had decreased metabolisms, slower brain waves, and reduced heart and respiratory rates during their meditation. Benson's evidence was quickly termed "the relaxation response." All he had to do after his profound evidence was to test the same hypothesis on medical students at Harvard. He quickly hit a snag when the students weren't showing the same response. Benson learned that untrained meditators didn't reach the same relaxation as trained individuals, so he tried something new.

Benson examined and researched various relaxation techniques from around the globe. Ancient cultures used meditation, yoga, breathing exercises, mantras, and prayers to relax their mind and body, but they were trained through self-practice. A lightbulb lit up, and Benson realized that there are two key factors to the relaxation response. The first is that it requires repetition of words, sounds, music, or movement, and the second was that it required the students to disregard other thoughts. He tried again by asking the students to only count to one this time, and they needed to repeat the number they were saying out loud. He also instructed them to return to the number every time they felt distracted. Using the number one is clever because it also doesn't act as a cue to ignite thought and memories for most people.

Benson was excited when he managed to induce the same relaxation response in the students as he did in the meditators. Finally, he had something measurable for science. His research has connected the relaxation response to numerous health improvements, including reduced blood pressure, stress, insomnia, depression, anxiety, arthritis symptoms, and infertility. Resting heart rate was also improved through the relaxation response, and the fight or flight response was reduced. Moreover, two of his main findings were that the relaxation response is an anti-aging mechanism, and it can switch genes on and off (Martin, 2008). Indeed, stress ages the body and mind, but the second piece of evidence changes the way we think about diseases.

The human body has approximately 40,000 genes, and faulty genes trigger diseases like various cancers, cystic fibrosis, sickle cell anemia, arthritis, diabetes, hypertension, Alzheimer's, and heart disease. Other genetic conditions include Turner syndrome, myoclonic epilepsy, and dementia. Regular use of the relaxation response promotes anti-inflammatory and antioxidant benefits, which Benson proved can change genomic activity in the human body. It doesn't matter what form you use; all that matters is that you practice the relaxation response for at least 20 minutes twice daily. The best time is early morning because the brain is still naturally running on slower waves. The relaxation response is often called a cure for hazardous stress response.

The parasympathetic nervous system is what you need to activate regularly to maintain balance in the mind-body connection. The relaxation response allows the PNS to perceive threats correctly, which means it won't trigger fight or flight unless necessary. The relaxation response is the deepest form of mind-body relaxation. So, how can we all benefit from the relaxation response? Benson, among others, have found a myriad of proven techniques to induce it.

Learning How to Relax

You're not reading this book for the sake of nothing. You're obviously reading it because you forgot how to relax just as most people have. It's not a weakness, but it has disadvantages, which you've learned about. Human beings will always lean toward survival and preservation, so there's nothing natural about relaxation if you don't intentionally practice it. The modern world doesn't make it easier for us to adopt the natural state, but it's part of your biology. It's madness to leave the PNS to become a white elephant when it's designed to help us. Meditation, breathing exercises, and yoga are some well-known methods, but there's a wide range of methods you can use to relax again, so waste no more time.

Meditation

Meditation is one of the greatest ways to reduce stress, and two types have particularly been designed to promote deep relaxation and the elimination of harmful thoughts and emotions. Allowing the body and mind to enter a state of utter serenity is good for every part of the mind-body connection. Benson's work paved the way for better living, and you can use a simple, step-by-step guide to enter his meditative state daily. Benson developed a guide to meditate for optimal activation of the relaxation response, and it includes all the requirements. Follow these steps to use his method of relaxation.

Step one is to close your eyes as you sit in a comfortable position, whether you're on the floor with your legs crossed or in a chair.

Follow this with an intentional relaxation of your muscles in step two, starting from the toes to the tip of your head. Tense each muscle group slightly and release them for better effect. Focus on one muscle group at a time. Toes are one group, calves are another, and the core muscles in your stomach are yet another individual group.

The third step is to use your nose to breathe in gently, and pay attention to your breath. Focus on how it makes your insides feel as the fresh air gets absorbed into your lungs.

The fourth step is to start a repetitive word or number on each breath you push out of your mouth. Use the word 'one' as you push the air out. Say it out loud for the best results, or repeat it in your mind.

Next, continue repeating this word as you feel more and more relaxed for 15 to 20 minutes. Don't be alarmed once you manage to master the relaxation response. You might be in this stage for longer than 20 minutes.

The final step is to open your eyes slowly but remain seated in your relaxed state for a little while before getting up. Pay attention to how relaxed you feel for a minute or two.

Don't be disappointed if you don't reach deep relaxation on your first few tries. It takes practice, and you'll improve with every session. Benson's methods also aren't the only form of meditation that promotes better well-being and reduced stress. His model was designed specifically to elicit the opposite response to stress, but another name has made great strides in meditation relaxation science. Professor Jon Kabat-Zinn from the University of Massachusetts Medical School is the founding father of the Mindfulness-Based Stress Reduction (MBSR) Institute and program. Benson and Kabat-Zinn have studied the differences in brain activity between their programs and others. Astonishingly, each program affects the brain and its functions differently.

Kabat-Zinn's model focuses on using mindfulness to achieve deeper relaxation by not being judgmental toward yourself and others and experiencing everything in the present moment. Both programs teach meditation, but mindfulness is more than a physical exercise. It's a mindset you adopt, and meditation is merely an intentional practice of it. Mindfulness teaches us that the past and future have no real influence over our current well-being. The only time and place you can make a difference are here and now. Anyway, a a istant professor of psychology at Harvard Medical School, Sara Lazar, also studied the differences between the two programs (Lazar, 2018). Healthy adults with high-stress levels were placed in one of the two programs for eight weeks.

One group was called the relaxation response program and the other one was the mindfulness program. Both groups showed phenomenal improvements in their stress reduction and overall mindfulness, but the MSBR program showed further benefits. The MBSR group showed higher compassion for themselves and others and lower rumination tendencies toward negative thoughts. The mindful group was instructed to pay attention to their awareness and acceptance during a body scan, without attempting to change anything. The relaxation response group had to intentionally relax their muscles during the body scan meditation. Both groups' brain activities were measured.

The relaxation response group showed improved activity in the inferior frontal gyrus and its supplementary motor regions, indicating that this group achieved higher control over their brain functions. They were able to deliberately control their brain functions more easily. The mindfulness group showed improved activity between the pregenual anterior cingulate and insula, indicating enhanced sensory awareness and perception. This proves that both programs worked in the brain, but on different levels. Mindfulness meditation improves sensory awareness, which gives you inner control over your thoughts and emotions. Relaxation meditation improves deliberate control mechanisms, which enables you to improve your behavioral reactions to the stressors.

Both programs offer unique contributions to your well-being, so it helps to practice both. Applying these meditation strategies to your daily life will encourage neuroplasticity in both of the highlighted regions. Mindful meditation is also simple if you follow a few steps.

Step one encourages you to become comfortable by closing your eyes and breathing evenly. Keep doing this until you feel more relaxed, which normally takes about two minutes.

Step two reminds you to use your awareness. You're already achieving this by paying attention to your bodily sensations and breath. Focus on how your body feels with every passing moment.

Step three is to open your awareness to thoughts and emotions. Allow them to come into your mind, and give them a chance to manifest as physical sensations. The only trick to this step is to not judge them, no matter what.

Step four intends to change your perception of these feelings. Notice how your thoughts and emotions are passing by slowly, but they're not in control of you. Let them gradually dissipate as you realize they're temporary.

Step five is to remind yourself that you remain in the present moment. Feel your body connect to the ground as you slowly open your eyes. Sit on this present space for a few moments before getting up.

Meditation in any form has benefits, but adopting these two types will prove beneficial to your health.

Yoga

Yoga is known as physical movements or asana. It's taken the western world by storm, and everyone's practicing flexibility to be able to reach their toes. However, yoga goes far deeper than physical flexibility. It's another practice of the mind-body connection that offers deep relaxation. Yoga is an antidote for the physiological changes in the body when you experience chronic or acute stress. The changes happen during your practice, and they continue beyond your stretches if you consistently use yoga. Muscular tension causes aches and pain, and yoga soothes the tension by stretching, strengthening, and easing the muscles.

The breathing exercises during yoga can also calm the mind and body by regulating your heart rate and oxygen levels to the brain. A brain that receives enough oxygen and nutrients reaches optimal focus and clarity, opposing the negative thoughts by awakening the logical mind. Yoga also elicits relaxation, which decreases the flurry of stress hormones in the body. Yoga ranges from gentle breathing and flow classes to more strenuous relaxation and stretching. The type you practice relies heavily on what you enjoy, but don't omit any types you haven't tried yet. Obviously, someone with advanced osteoarthritis and fragile bones will use flow meditation, but someone trying to strengthen and relax their muscles might prefer progressive classes.

Yoga requires three aspects to work for better health. The poses called asana must be combined with controlled breathing and a brief period of meditation. Meditation is achieved simply by holding your pose for 60 seconds at a time. Each factor can also be practiced alone, but combining them is what makes yoga a potent stress reducer that leads to less anxiety, depression, and physiological health changes. Yogic breathing can be achieved at your desk or in an elevator. Use your diaphragm to draw a deep and controlled breath into your nose, hold it for a moment, and release it slowly and completely. Repeat this five times, and you've completed a yogic breathing exercise. Add a simple side-bend to offer physical stretching when you feel overwhelmed by stress.

For the side bend, place both arms over your head, and grab one elbow with the other one. Bend slightly and slowly to the opposite direction of your held elbow, and bring yourself back up slowly. Breath in every time you bend down to your side and release the breath when you center yourself again. Do these another five times on each side, and you're practicing yoga on the go.

Yoga is a fun experience and social booster, and it provides medical benefits, too. According to Harvard Health Publishing (2009), various forms of yoga have vast health benefits beyond stress reduction. You can lower your blood pressure, maintain better glucose and insulin levels in diabetes, and prevent heart disease. It's an all-round winner.

Reverting to stress for a moment, yoga has also proven to be highly effective in the treatment of post-traumatic stress (PTS). Keep in mind that PTS and post-traumatic stress disorder (PTSD) are different conditions. The former kind is an acute response after severe stress or trauma. It happens immediately after a car accident or getting a call to say that someone passed away. The onset of these symptoms is fast, and it normally lasts up to a month. In many cases, PTS isn't severe enough to ward treatment, but in some cases, it's severe enough to mirror PTSD symptoms. PTSD is a more severe and prolonged condition triggered by trauma. It's persistent in interfering with your ability to function daily, and it typically lasts more than a month.

PTS can lead to PTSD, but the latter doesn't need the former to develop. The common trigger between the two conditions is trauma, but PTS being a precursor and risk for PTSD, meaning you need to manage traumatic stress immediately. Treatment is offered if your symptoms are severe, but maintaining a healthy mental state is essential through relaxation exercises to prevent PTSD from manifesting. Severe enough symptoms of either condition include rumination of traumatic events and emotions. You might suffer from nightmares, and physical symptoms are common.

Insomnia, irritability, and a constant fear or paranoia are also severe symptoms. Fear triggers the fight or flight mode, and the longer you remain in this daily fluctuation, the more the immune system malfunctions.

Returning yourself to a normal state while you're in shock and paranoia is complex. Fortunately, yoga has proven to return PTS and PTSD sufferers to their base state during severe shock or paranoia (Minded Institute, n.d.). Experiencing trauma disconnects the mind and body, and yoga reconnects them. Being aware during your yoga practices can already bring you back to the present moment. Learning to ground yourself in the present moment by moving your body in repetitive motions that get your oxygen flowing back to the brain helps to bring you out of shock. Don't wait until you experience trauma before you practice yoga. Practice it now by signing up for classes to learn proper poses and breathing so you can face the shock that comes with severely triggered stress.

Breathing Techniques

Breathing is more than just a life force; it's also a method to relax the mind-body connection. There are two kinds of breathing that make a difference. The first kind is focused breathing. This is similar to what you used in the "desk or elevator" example. You can stand, sit, or lie down as you close your eyes and simply pay attention to your breath. You don't need to control it in focused breathing. You must simply focus on how the air passes through you, into you, and out of you. Follow the air as your diaphragm pulls it deeper, and notice how it feels. Don't even attempt to control the air. Paying attention to your breathing is the easiest exercise for relaxation.

The second kind of breathing is called controlled breathing, which is an umbrella type for various exercises, one of which is boxed breathing. This technique is even used by paramedics when they respond to accident scenes. Start by closing your eyes and counting to four while you evenly pull your breath into your nose. Hold the air for another count of four, and slowly exhale for the final count of four. Boxed breathing can also be repeated as many times as you need to relax. It's useful for shock and fear.

Another controlled breathing technique is called alternate nostril breathing, which is inspired by ancient yogic practices. Combining this technique with boxed breathing can bring deep relaxation to your mind and body. However, alternate nostril breathing requires a little finesse and practice. Follow the steps to achieve it.

Start by sitting comfortably and closing your eyes.

Fold your middle fingers so your thumb and pinky fingers are facing outward.

Place your thumb on one nostril, and your pinky against your forehead.

Inhale for four seconds through the open nostril, and hold the breath for another four seconds.

Alternate nostrils with your thumb, and allow the air to push out of your open nostril for four seconds.

Start the process with your now open nostril before alternating to the other one again.

Repeat this exercise six times.

Breathing is a natural ability of the human body, but sometimes, we can use breathing exercises to calm the worst of emotions.

Meditation Guidance

Body scan meditation is one of the simplest and most effective meditation types. Use this simple guide to practice a body scan.

Lie flat on a bed, and close your eyes. Use focused breathing for two minutes to relax before the scan.

Once relaxed, bring your attention to your head or feet to start the scan. Notice the sensations you feel in your feet while you continue to focus on your breathing. Don't give the sensations any labels. Just focus on them as you stay in this region for five seconds.

Move your attention up to your ankles, and keep focusing on the sensations in this area for another five seconds. Notice the sensations in the muscles of your ankles before you move to the calves.

Stick to each region for five seconds before moving one joint higher. Pay special attention to the sensations in the abdomen, chest, and head.

You can also repeat the exercise in reverse once you reach your opposite point.

Open your eyes when you're ready and remain in the silence and relaxation before you stretch your muscles when you get up.

Body scan aside, progressive muscle relaxation (PMR) is another great meditation technique you can use. It follows similar guidelines to a body scan, except you'll be tensing each muscle group slightly before abruptly releasing it. Pull muscles tighter and pay attention to the relief you experience when you feel a sudden release. Scan, tense, and release each muscle group at least once, and don't forget to include your arms and hands. Tensing the face is as simple as pulling funny faces, sticking your tongue out, or you can raise your eyebrows high. Combine the body scan guide with the muscle relaxation tools to use PMR, which requires more practice than body scans. Keep doing it daily for four weeks before expecting major results.

The meditation type that requires the most practice is mindful meditation. The awareness and perception you need require you to find a meditation spot void of any distractions and interruptions. Let's guide you through it.

Once distractions are removed, find a comfortable place to sit quietly and straighten your spine. Your spine must be straight, which doubles as a yoga pose.

Choose a focal point, whether it's the air moving in your nose and out of your mouth or a spot on the wall.

Using a word also helps you achieve the relaxation response, such as repeating the word 'one.'

The entire session requires you to keep focusing on your focal point, even when distractions flow in and out of your mind. Allow thoughts to run their course, and bring your attention back to your word.

Maintain your focus as you offer no judgment to anything that tries to distract you. You can stay in this state for 15 to 20 minutes.

Sticking to a focal point and removing distractions is harder than you think, so keep practicing it.

Simple Techniques

Other than breathing exercises, there are a few more simpler techniques you can use to activate the relaxation response. The first trick you can use is to adopt a "let it happen" or passive attitude when distractions flurry your mind in meditation or any experience. Choose to focus on a mantra, such as 'om.' Allow the sound to resonate for a while with every repetition, and keep focusing on the vibrations in your throat. Let distractions come, but keep your focus on your mantra. Distractions will interfere, especially when you're new to meditation or mindfulness. You can teach your mind that you're in control by practicing a passive attitude.

The second simple technique is to make yourself comfortable. Nothing brings relaxation like a comfortable armchair or even a bed. Sit down, and relax your arms next to you. Allow your feet to relax against the floor, and use PMR to force the rest of your body to relax if resistance is a problem. Close your eyes and intentionally remain in this comfortable state against the floor and chair for 15 minutes. Use your passive attitude to handle distractions when your comfort levels are disturbed. Give your mind time to slow down and relax. It's not used to doing this, so you need to practice it as much as possible. Make sure the chair you use is comfortable, and relaxation will come naturally.

Mantras or repetitive phrases give you a strong focal point because you can hear and feel it, which makes them another great trick to activate the relaxation response. Stand straight with your feet embedded into the ground, and choose any word or phrase that offers personal attachment and creates physical sensations. You can keep your eyes open, or you can close them. You can repeat the name of someone you love. Voice their name out loud, and pay attention to the feelings of the sound resonance. Focus on how the sound of their name brings comfort to you, and how it might make you feel happy or sleepy.

Visualization

Visualization is used to change your focus to something more pleasant when you feel stressed or anxious, or it can be practiced to inspire yourself for future goals. The trick with visualization for stress reduction is that you use your imagination to paint a picture to change your emotional state. The scene you choose to paint must calm you and make you feel comfortable. You can also use imagery from places you visited that offered relaxation, such as beaches, forests, and mountain hikes. Follow these steps, and you'll ignite the relaxation response.

Step one is to enter a calmer state of mind with meditation or a breathing exercise of your choice. Close your eyes and choose something to focus on.

Step two is to imagine a picture forming in front of you. Be as vivid as possible, and use as many details, shapes, and colors as you can. Give yourself a few moments to paint the whole picture. Let's say you're painting a beach. Add details for the sand, color changes for the waves crashing in and out, and the brightness of the sun. Imagine a bird flying over the waves, looking for fish under the water. Bring people into your imagination, especially people you enjoy and who make you relax.

Step three is to experience the visualization completely with all five senses in your imagined picture. Feel the sand tickling your toes as the waves gently wash over them, changing the temperature against your skin. Listen to the waves further out as they move over each other gently. Watch the bird scanning the water for fish, and listen to the sounds of your loved ones giggling around the sandcastle. Feel the warmth of the sun touch your skin, and taste the salt in the air.

Step four is to bring yourself back to your meditation position slowly. Allow the imagined picture to fade slowly as you come back by counting your breaths from three to one. Use the Mississippi counts, and keep sitting in your relaxed position when your eyes open. Pay attention to how this visualization has changed the way your body and mind feel.

Visualization might not be easy at first, but you can use a guided meditation session that falls under the Yoga Nidra practice. Look specifically for Yoga Nidra sessions because they combine visualization, breathing techniques, meditation, and focal guidance.

Physical Techniques

Some physical strategies can trigger the relaxation response in your brain. The first trick is to give yourself a massage. Self-massage is a valuable technique that offers sensory changes to your environment that allows relaxation to start. You can use a five-minute self-massage to reduce stress and release tension in your muscles.

Start with your neck and shoulders by kneading the back of them. Roll a loose fist gently across your neck and shoulders.

Move to the base of your neck by making tiny circle movements with your thumbs.

Work your way up the skull by gently massaging it under your hair.

Stop massaging, and start tapping your fingers against the skull, moving downward again.

Now, start at the bottom of your face, and make tiny circular motions with your fingertips.

Move to the cheeks and pay special attention to the muscles here.

Keep making circular movements against your temples, and move to your forehead.

Use your middle fingers to make the same movements over your nose as you continue massaging your forehead.

Finally, close your eyes and cover them with your hands while you breathe slowly and evenly for a while.

A self-massage can be achieved on any part of your body. Don't hesitate to use it when you feel stressed.

Rhythmic movements also offer repetition that promotes relaxation, especially when you do them mindfully. Don't think of it as exercise but rather as a flow of motion and repetition. Useful exercises include rowing, walking, running, swimming, dancing, and climbing. Bring mindfulness into the movements by paying attention to how your foot feels every time it hits the ground. It creates sensations in the foot that travel up the leg through your muscles. Focus on the release of these sensations when your foot rises again, and move your attention to your other foot when it hits the ground. It's possible to find mindfulness and relaxation in the simplest of experiences.

Another physical technique commonly used for relaxation is tai chi. It's the slowest form of self-defense, but it comes with rhythm and focused coordination. Sign up for classes so you can coordinate your slow, flowing movements of the body with others. Tai chi is also a low-impact routine that offers benefits to any fitness level and age. You'll learn to sync your breathing and movements as your body flows back and forth.

Relaxation is an incredible art to master. You already have the biological tool to use it; you must simply practice it now. Schedule daily time for various relaxation techniques. Moreover, expect it to be hard at first. Most of these techniques require practice, but so does anything worthwhile in life. You've gathered the tools you need to practice positive experiences, and now you'll learn about the internal changes needed and how to make them happen.

Chapter 5:

Placebo and Nocebo Effect: When Negative Thinking Affects Your Health

Everyone tells you to look toward a brighter future or to think about improved health, especially when you first get diagnosed with a condition. There's some truth to what they say. Thoughts and emotions give way to poor health, but having a negative mindset can prevent you from improving your health. Your mindset is closely connected to the improvement or decline of your condition. It's time to learn about nocebo and placebo effects and how powerful they can be.

The Placebo Paradox

Do a little experiment before learning about the placebo effect. Walk up to someone, whether they're a friend or stranger, and behave concerned for a moment. Ask them if they feel fine because they look a little pale and hot under the collar. Give the person a minute or two to respond to your random query. Even strangers will respond if your acting skills are good enough to look genuinely concerned. The person might turn pale, even if they weren't before. They'll present symptoms after someone else shows concern that they don't look too well. It takes seconds for the person to move beyond their pre-chat condition to your perceived state of their health. They might even tell you that they don't feel so good, even if they were laughing and feeling great seconds earlier. The human mind is gullible from the inside and outside.

You can gladly tell the person that it was merely an experiment so they don't feel sick for no reason, but you've just activated a negative placebo effect in someone when you made them feel unwell by telling them they look sick. The placebo effect is a powerful medical tool, even though sometimes it provides no treatment. Placebos are any medical treatments or diagnoses that appear to be real, but they contain no active ingredients to change your health or symptoms. They can be pills, shots, or any form of fake medical treatment that offers no genuine health changes, yet somehow, people experience changes in their condition. Some people have positive symptoms where their condition improves with the fake treatment, and others have negative symptoms from the placebo when their condition worsens.

Another negative outcome from placebo is when people develop side effects from treatment that can't cause it. Placebo and nocebo effects are strong contenders to support the mind-body connection. Placebos are highly effective in clinical trials to help researchers test new treatments. New drugs have to go through rigorous tests to determine their efficiency and positive effect on existing conditions, such as cholesterol, diabetes, and asthma. Studies are always divided into two or more groups. One group receives the new drug, and the other group receives a placebo that looks the same. None of the participants will know whether they received the real or placebo drug, but both groups will be told that their bad cholesterol will decrease as one example. Researchers compare the placebo and the new drug results to determine whether it works or not.

These placebo tests also expose side effects. Some researchers find control groups who mirror similar effects to the real groups. They believed that their cholesterol will decrease, and some control participants experience improvement. They might also experience some weird side effects, especially if they've conveniently been warned that it might happen. Give someone a drug, and tell them that it will regulate their glucose levels better, but it might cause night sweats. Suddenly, the person's waking up in a pool of sweat every night, but their glucose levels seem better. The reason why placebos work in most cases is that it tricks our expectations, and the mind-body connection listens to our expectations. If you expect to lower your glucose levels, chances are you will because your brain is following your instructions.

Always remember your body, immune system, and mind have no connection to the external world, and you have to provide experiences for them. A doctor who spent many years studying medicine has told you that this tablet will prevent insulin spikes and cause night sweats, so your expectations rely on an expert who knows better. The brain sees this as instructions to work toward the outcome an expert shared. The body's chemistry can change to mimic the effects of real medications with your expectations. Expectations have a strong influence on how you perceive something in psychology. Your expectations are cued by three factors, namely verbal, actions, and social. Verbal is the expert who tells you that you're going to feel like this and experience that.

Actions are simply applied by taking medication to make you feel better. The social factor was what your experiment proved. The tone of someone's voice matters, whether it's a doctor or someone in the street. That's why you need to have a concerning tone of voice for the experiment. Body language and eye contact also assert reassurance or concern. You can also try the experiment on someone with the flu and see how their symptoms improve as you keep telling them they look great. You're automatically giving someone clues as to how they must react, and it's amplified when these clues come from a medical expert. The second reason why the placebo effect works psychologically is that it offers association or conditioning. Your brain is wired to associate certain cues with specific outcomes.

For example, you eat prawns for the first time, and you get sick because it was cooked wrong. Your mind automatically associates prawns with feeling sick, making you avoid it in the future. Conditioning is how your brain learns, and these associations will influence your behavior. People generally associate doctors with feeling better. They also associate with medication for migraines and fevers. The pill only needs to look similar. It doesn't even need to contain any substances used to affect your physiological chemistry. One of the main uses of placebos is to reduce pain. This can also result from the chemicals and endorphins released in the brain when you expect or associate medication with reduced pain. Endorphins are natural pain-killers that act similarly to morphine.

The elevation of positive neurotransmitters enhances your mood, regulates your emotions, increases your awareness, and controls the way you react to pain and other symptoms. The placebo effect goes beyond positive thinking and well-conditioned expectations. You might only require one factor of expectations to be met. The Department of Neurology at Harvard Medical School examined the power of the placebo effect on patients who knew what it was (Kam-Hansen et al., 2014). Three groups of participants suffering from osteoarthritis pain were used. One group was given medication to reduce the pain, and another group was given nothing.

The placebo group was given medication that clearly read 'placebo' on the label. The first group successfully reduced pain symptoms, and the second group wasn't very successful. However, the placebo group was 50% as successful in reducing pain as the genuine medication group. Kam-Hansen and his associates realized we only need to meet one of the three factors to associate our expectations with an outcome. Taking a pill daily is already conditioned to associate with feeling better. Magnetic resonance scans were also used to determine how the brain activates during a placebo trial. Patients showed higher levels of activation in the frontal gyrus region of the brain after taking a placebo drug. This region makes up a third of your frontal lobe, which happens to be the same place where higher or conscious thinking occurs.

Placebos might not completely depress advanced conditions; however, they change the way our brain responds to illness and its symptoms on a chemical level. Your nature and understanding of the disease help, and so does your belief in how effective the treatment will be. The type of response you expect from your doctor, and the way the doctor conveys the efficiency and positive outlook of the treatment will improve your chances of recovery. The final factor that contributes to the placebo effect being more effective is genetic. People with genes leaning toward the pursuit of more dopamine and rewards are also more likely to benefit from a placebo effect. Indeed, positive mindsets are stronger when they're genetically adopted, but we still have classical conditioning on our sides, meaning we can teach the brain to associate positive outcomes with certain cues.

The placebo effect can be used to decrease your symptoms related to certain health conditions, and it can help you to take greater strides toward recovery because you believe your treatment will work. Your beliefs, your perception of the world, and the expectation you hold over recovery are what stand between you and better living. Learn about the most prominent evidence supporting placebo effects to enhance your belief in a simple method of taking back control.

Placebo Studies

There's empirical evidence of the placebo effect and mind-body connections. Pain reduction is one of the main focuses of placebos, but studies have also covered other symptoms from more severe conditions. Cancer patients are prone to fatigue during their treatment and after. A randomized clinical study was published in *The Scientific Reports Journal* that focused on how placebo trials affect cancer patients (Hoenemeyer et al., 2018). Seventy-four cancer survivors with chronic fatigue were placed on a 21-day program. One group continued their regular treatment, and the other group was placed on a placebo drug labeled as such. The placebo group knew what they were using.

The regular group was also offered a 21-day placebo treatment after the initial three weeks of normal treatment. The results were profoundly in favor of placebo treatment. The group that used placebo treatment in the first three weeks were showing improved symptoms, even more than the traditional treatment provided to the other group. Moreover, they continued to show improvements over the three weeks after discontinuing the placebo drug. The second group reported the same improvements after switching from regular treatment to placebo drugs in the second 21-day stretch. This study proves how our brains can be tricked into feeling and behaving better, even when we're aware of the trickery.

Another study was published in *The JAMA Psychiatry Journal* (Pecina et al., 2015). It focused on depression and the alleviation of its symptoms. Thirty-five depressed participants were divided into two groups. None of them were on any antidepressant medication at the time, but the first group was given a placebo drug labeled as a fast-acting antidepressant, and the other group was given a drug labeled as a placebo. Furthermore, the group taking the so-called antidepressant received a placebo shot at the end of the week, and the other group didn't. The group who received shots were also told that their mood will improve, and both groups were then scanned using a positron emission tomography (PET) scanner.

A PET scan uses dye in your bloodstream to examine your body for diseases. The tracers in the dye will show your doctor how well your brain or other organs are functioning. The groups were then switched around for the second week, and another PET scan was completed on the mirrored groups at the end of the week. This study concluded that participants in both weeks were showing symptom improvements in their brain scans. Depression was reduced, and brain activity in the regions that control stress and emotional regulation was enhanced. Looking at these two studies, you can see that knowing about the placebo or not will already influence your mind.

A placebo effect is also not considered a cure, but your mindset can change the chemistry of your body and brain, leading to positive symptom relief and faster recovery from an illness. Many medications also only target symptoms, so knowing you can control your pain and fatigue with your expectations and conditioning is a win.

The Nocebo Paradox

The opposite reaction to the placebo effect is the nocebo effect, which already happened if you managed to make someone feel sick for no reason in your experiment. Did they turn pale, or did you make them feel light-headed? This is the nocebo effect. A nocebo effect happens when the placebo effect turns into phantom symptoms in the case of your experiment, but it can also turn your outcome negative when the doctor tells you that you might gain a few pounds while taking a certain drug. The nocebo effect works on the same principles as the placebos do. Your expectations, the way your doctor explains potential side effects, and your association between certain medications making you nauseous can make the symptoms manifest in real-time.

It also ignites a physiological and chemical reaction in your body. Sometimes, you can suffer from negative side effects from a treatment that contains no substances to make you feel sick because you don't trust your doctor. We tend to do that. We go to the same doctor for many years, and we continue going to them, even when they lose our trust. It's a human flaw because we hate change, and finding a new physician is a change. Other factors that influence a nocebo effect is the cost of the treatment or medication. However, the groundwork of your conditioning lies in the same expectations, communication with your doctor, and your associations with the health condition or treatment.

Someone who lost a close loved one to cancer might not have the most positive outlook on the condition, even if their treatment is working fine. Their symptoms might decline their quality of life because they have no faith in themselves to overcome the condition. Their self-belief is damaged, and this influences their expectations negatively. What makes them more capable of responding to treatment if their once healthy sister succumbed to cancer? Take pain medication as another example. You've always used the same medication prescribed by your doctor, but you haven't had time to refill your prescription. Online drug stores allow you to have something delivered to your home, so you research a few options and click on the "add to cart" button. You feel brain fog and fatigue a few days later, and you examine the package insert.

One symptom stands out clearly. This medication might cause drowsiness. Make a doctor's appointment and take the medication along. The doctor points out that the medications have the same components and possible side effects. In this case, you've trusted your doctor to give you medication without side effects, but you can't trust online drug stores. The only fault here is that you didn't compare package inserts, and that's how the symptoms have occurred. The same thing happens with topical eczema creams. The drug store ran out of your brand, so you asked for a similar brand instead. Suddenly, the cream feels different, and it stings your skin as you rub it on. However, you'll realize that the only difference is the brand name. You simply didn't read the potential side effects of your usual cream.

One of the biggest problems facing nocebo effects is that doctors and pharmaceutical companies need to ethically advise patients of potential side effects. Potential is the big word of the day. To be approved, medications need to meet the standards of the Food and Drug Administration (FDA), which requires companies to list possible side effects. Ethically, a doctor also needs to warn you about them. The difference lies in how the doctor explains it. Nevertheless, the nocebo effect is as prevalent in the mind-body connection as its positive counterpart. It's a combination of experiences, expectations, beliefs, and mindset. It ranges from psychology to chemistry, and there's enough evidence to support it as well.

Nocebo Studies

A nocebo effect happens when the treatment makes you feel worse, increasing symptoms like pain and fatigue. However, this effect can manifest if your mindset is negative and your beliefs are guided by the wrong conditioning. A study published by the Department of Algesiology at Georg-August University in Germany shows evidence of the nocebo effect (Pfingstein et al., 2001). Fifty patients who suffered from chronic lower back pain participated in a flexibility-style treatment. Researchers wanted to determine whether the anticipation of pain would induce fear-related behaviors, particularly avoidance. The first group of participants was informed that the simple leg-flexing task wouldn't increase their existing pain. The second group was casually informed that the exercise could cause increased pain.

Both groups also had to complete fear-avoidance questionnaires and pain disability indices before the test. The information from these questionnaires was factored into the results, including the participant's current range of motion and flexibility. Each participant was asked to express their pain and fear at the time of the test as well, and they had to indicate how unpleasant the experiment was after the task was completed. The results showed nocebo effects across the variables applied to the experiment. People who anticipated pain and were informed of an increase in it were performing less, and they experienced more pain and fear during the task. This result shows that our behavioral performance can change, depending on our fears and beliefs. The nocebo effect can take your anticipation or expectations and turn them into real symptoms.

Another study published by the University of Florence in Italy examined the nocebo effect from a different angle (Mondaini et al., 2007). Finasteride 5 mg was used to test the effects of negative symptoms manifesting in patients under placebo controls. This drug is commonly used for the alleviation of symptoms related to prostate problems. It also comes with a list of potential side effects on the package insert. One-hundred and twenty patients with prostate hyperplasia participated in a 12-month study. The patients were equally divided into two groups. The first group was prescribed this drug, and they were told that it might cause erectile dysfunction, lower libido, and problems with ejaculation, which are genuine concerns for this drug.

They were informed of the symptoms, but the researcher also said they hardly ever occur. The second group was given the same medication, and they weren't informed properly about the potential side effects. Only 15% of the uninformed group suffered from erectile dysfunction, but a whopping 44% of the conditioned group suffered from it. Sometimes, ignorance truly is bliss when it comes to medical treatments. Ignorance allows you to avoid knowing what medications can do, and once again, the main focus is the word 'can.' No medication comes with definite side effects. Every side effect is merely a possibility. Indeed, your doctor will inform you of the potential side effects if they're ethical, but you need to realize that these effects are rare and uncommon.

Anyway, the nocebo effect is far more powerful than we imagine. Would you believe that it's powerful enough to kill someone? The Veterans Affairs Medical Center in Jackson, Mississippi, published a shocking case study (Reeves et al., 2007). A young man of 26 was unaware that he was already part of a psychiatric placebo study. He was prescribed antidepressants to combat his emotional instability when he decided to end his life. He took 29 placebo antidepressants, hoping to commit suicide. This isn't the fascinating part. What struck the fascination of the researchers was that his vitals went mad, even though the medication could not make him sick. This young man believed that he was dying, which sent his vitals into chaos.

His blood pressure dropped to dangerous lows, and he required fluids to keep him alive until he could be informed of the placebo drug. To no surprise, the young man quickly recovered from his near-death experience as soon as he learned about the trickery of his prescribed medication. Sadly, the antidepressant placebo wasn't working, considering that he tried to commit suicide. However, the nocebo effect nearly made him successful. What shocks the medical world about this case is that this young man believed so much in the medication that he assumed it would kill him. His belief was strong enough to drive his expectations toward biochemical changes in his body.

This case study opened the door to many others because it's crucial for doctors to understand how the nocebo effect can play out when they diagnose, medicate, or treat people. It's sad to think a young man nearly lost his life to 'candy.' Negative effects aside, you can change your outlook toward recovery and the management of your conditions simply by being aware of the influence your expectations and previous conditioning have over your mind-body connection. Your conscious mind is what controls your thought habits, and your belief systems influence the patterns you use. Start believing you can face your symptoms and overcome them, and you will.

Stop focusing on the potential side effects, and make sure your doctor is using positive body language and tone when they discuss the potential effects with you. One simple method you can use to stop this negative cycle and belief system is to determine how rare side effects can be. Do some research if you want to understand the rarity of negative outcomes. Stop focusing on pain, stings, burns, and the bad stuff because, in most cases, these side effects aren't common. Rather make a conscious decision to think positively about your condition and health in general. Choose the placebo effect over the nocebo effect as you've learned that it can make a difference, even if you know about it.

It doesn't mean you must stop your medication. Placebo effects work best on relieving symptoms and improving your recovery journey. They don't cure you, but they make your journey far more pleasant, irrespective of what condition you suffer from. To enhance your overall health, you also need to learn about the theory behind challenges and threats, which is coming next.

Chapter 6:

A Theory of Challenge and Threat

The ability of the mind-body connection to keep your health at peak levels and to manage symptoms better lies within a theory that distinguishes threats from challenges. Your brain needs to learn to distinguish one from the other, and this will make a way for better living. Both responses trigger separate reactions in your body and brain, meaning you can switch the threatening response off when you feel like leading a stress-free life instead of drowning in chemical and biological responses that rip your health to shreds. Adopting a mindset that perceives challenges can also bring many benefits to your life.

The Truth About Perceptions

Mindsets matter, and so does your perception of what lies in front of you. Changing your view can open new doors, reduce stress, lay new pathways through neuroplasticity, and turn nocebo effects into placebo effects. The biopsychosocial model of challenge and threat (BPS) is another area of study that confirms the existence of the mind-body connection and how you can use it to change your outlook on life and health, ultimately changing your outcomes. A review of this model was published in *The Social and Personality Psychology Compass Journal*, which proves that we can control the response in our brain and our heart's functions to prevent the negative consequences of stress and wrongful perceptions (Seery, 2013). The evidence shows that our psychological responses can lead to certain patterns in cardiovascular reactions.

Stress is the common driver between the two responses when we have to achieve something, pursue a goal, improve our health, or take on a new challenge. This area of research also focused mainly on the proactive pursuit of goals and the performance enhancement of athletes because the psychological response is hard to measure in other situations. However, measuring the activity changes in the heart leads to specific outcomes when people are actively involved in an experience. It's been known for a long time that stress triggers cardiovascular changes. There are two kinds of stress, but the theory of challenge and threat measures your responses to stress if you perceive it as a threat or challenge. In simple terms, everything we face is either a threat or a challenge.

Our mind perceives a task as a challenge if we have enough resources to overcome the demand. For example, an athlete receives an email inviting him to a marathon. He experiences cardiovascular changes when he opens it. His heart will beat faster, and he'll experience a jolt of adrenaline when he thinks about the wind brushing his face as he sprints toward the finish line. He has what he needs to reach the goal of this scenario. The demand is that he must be fit enough to run 20 miles, and his training shows that he can do this.

On the other hand, the athlete could perceive this email as a threat because it came from his manager. He doesn't want to let his manager down, but his cardiovascular changes are heading in the opposite direction. He doesn't have what it takes to complete the marathon because he twisted his ankle last week. It's a matter of supply and demand. The situation presents itself as having so much demand, and your skills, resources, and abilities offer the supply. The challenge becomes a threat if the supply can't meet the demand. However, the athlete's perception of whether he can meet the demand is crucial, too. Let's say he has a negative belief about himself. He's never run 20 miles before, and his training hasn't brought him any closer. So, he'll perceive that he doesn't have enough supply. Our perceptions are often curated by our expectations, childhood, and social influence. Not having social support can also make us feel like we don't have the supply.

Being raised in a home where we're never good enough can install beliefs that we don't have what it takes. Our expectations are our own or that of society. If this athlete is assuming that he can't meet the demand unless he achieves perfection or first place, he won't experience the good side of stress, which is a challenge to push himself to greater things. Either way, a challenge is perceived when you must complete a task, whether it's improving your health or losing a few pounds to maintain better glucose levels, and your ability to decide whether it's a challenge is determined by your evaluation of low demand and high supply. Threats are perceived when you feel like the demand is too high and your supply is too low.

The review showed that your cardiovascular system responds to both, even if there are major differences. Threats increase your heart rate, blood pressure, and negative stress response. Your heart experiences vasoconstriction, which is the constriction of blood vessels to decrease blood flow to other organs, including the brain. Your cardiovascular system runs at a decreased efficiency. Your brain receives less oxygen, and it activates the negative stress response, releasing cortisol and adrenaline into your body at high rates. Your blood sugar elevates to provide you with energy, but negative emotions are flooding your mind and brain, wreaking havoc on every system. Brain fog, lost focus, impaired decision-making, and general cognitive decline take place.

Running your stress appraisal through distorted perceptions filter out any good biochemical reactions. This process can even make simple obstacles look like mountains. Driving to work becomes a constant threat, making it a daily struggle. Our perceptions also guide our anticipation, and this causes more problems. You won't perform if you're anticipating harm. You also won't see opportunities or improvements in the grey lines between black and white if your evaluation is faulty. Even worse, you can't respond to a threat if you're frozen with anticipated fear. Keep in mind that threats are more likely to push you into chronic stress, which keeps your blood vessels constricted, leading to many health problems.

Chronic pain, dementia, stroke, ulcers, fatigue, obesity, depression, anxiety, and digestive issues are waiting around the corner of anticipation and faulty perceptions. Perceiving threats where it doesn't exist can also lead to a shorter life. Elissa Epel and her associates (2004) studied genetic mutations and changes in people with negative or faulty perceptions. Every gene has telomere strands extending from it, and Epel's research found shorter strands in people who perceive small stressors as threats, indicating a shorter life span. You require longer telomere strands to live a longer life. This is the bad news that comes with negative evaluations regarding stress.

Seeing stressful or different situations as a challenge has proven to have vastly different cardiovascular effects in the review. Challenges increase the efficiency of your heart because vasodilation occurs when you're excited by the task or health goal. Vasodilation is when your blood vessels dilate enough to improve circulation throughout your body and brain. Every muscle and the brain itself is receiving ample amounts of oxygen to perform at their best. Challenges prepare you for success, and your focus, decision-making, coordination, and accuracy multiply. You experience positive emotions instead, and your entire mind-body connection functions better.

Indeed, the adrenal glands still release adrenaline and cortisol, but they also release oxytocin, which is something most people are unaware of. Keep in mind that your evaluation must lead to a perceived challenge to achieve the release of oxytocin. Challenged stress gives you the focus and energy to succeed. The reason for this is that stress is simply a message or signal that something you care about is at risk. Stress isn't bad in itself. It's only the way you translate the message to your brain and body. Other than the energy you receive and the motivation you grasp when you see a challenge, the release of oxytocin has many benefits. Oxytocin is the love hormone, or in this case, it's the hormone that pushes you to seek help when you need it. Sometimes, you'll face challenges that become threatening because you don't have the resources to manage them alone.

Social connections make us stronger, and they offer improved health. However, the release of this hormone that motivates us to seek assistance from our social support network also helps us gather the resources we need. We drop our guards, and we speak about our fears. We look for comfort in the place we often find it. Oxytocin also reduces negative feelings, and it suppresses the cortisol in your body, allowing you to return to the relaxation response you need after evaluating a situation. Once relaxed, you can better deal with the situation. Oxytocin also increases our pain threshold, and it promotes healing and growth. Often, the last thing we think about in times of dire stress is to turn to someone for help. Human beings are stubborn in that sense.

The connection between people builds emotional resilience in the face of stress. A study published by the University of Buffalo, New York, confirms that we can use this oxytocin release to manage our negative emotions better (Poulin and Holman, 2013). Reduce your negative emotions and you'll be evaluating the situation better, allowing you to turn your placebo effect on. Rising to challenges also promotes what's known as 'hormesis.' This is the gradual resilience you develop when you continually expose yourself to small amounts of stress. For example, challenging your weight loss goals to reduce insulin resistance can be achieved by pushing yourself a little harder each week. The challenges don't need to be exorbitant, either.

The first week might only require you to cut bread from your diet, and the second week is where you reduce artificial sweeteners, but the third week is where you start a short exercise routine daily. Steps make strides when they accumulate, and this allows you to constantly challenge yourself with simpler tasks that lead to success. There's one major danger to watch out for with challenges though. Don't allow yourself to become addicted to the endless pursuit of igniting this positive stress. Gambling addicts, workaholics, and exercise addicts are known to do this. Healthy challenges can become threats if it leads to addictive behaviors.

Doing what you love combined with the constant releases of dopamine triggers addictive behaviors, and many of them are harmful. However, the bottom line is that your perception of stress can be good or bad, and it can lead to desired or unwanted outcomes.

Taking Control of Your Perceptions

It always starts by being aware of the fault before taking action to change it. Awareness allows you to consciously make changes, and your perceptions are where you start. Think of it as mind over matter because you want to reshape the arousal system for each type of perception. Challenges need positive arousals, and threats require negative arousals. It can't be simpler than thinking differently about stress. See it in a new light, and force your mind to follow your direction. Your subconscious mind still can't process information that your conscious mind and senses haven't considered. Take the time you need to reappraise situations before you assume they're stressful.

T D artment of Psychology at Harvard University published evidence that only our appraisals can change our arousals over time (Jamieson et al., 2012). Harvard examined three groups of participants in their study. The first group was conditioned to rethink their stress surrounding a test, the second group was told to focus on how complicated the task was, and the last group was given no instructions. The group asked to reappraise their stress showed significant flexibility and adaptation in their stress levels, whereas the other two groups showed negative effects. This study also proved that we tend to perceive stress negatively through our underlying bias.

The second part of rethinking your stress is to consider how you value the outcome or event. You're more likely to transform your threats to challenges if you value the improvement, task, or change. How much does it mean to you? Perhaps, you're struggling with asthma. Your life hasn't been so great because you can't be active with your children. Changing this, turning the improvement of your condition into a challenge so it doesn't feel threatening anymore offers intrinsic motivation and purpose. You'd love to play ball with your kids, and you can't wait until you no longer need an inhaler every time you must chase them.

Learn to respond differently to events and situations that offer genuine challenges to improve your health. A pounding heart only means you're prepared for action. Rapid breathing is increasing the flow of oxygen to your brain, and surging blood gets the oxygen to every organ and muscle. This is how you reach your peak and challenge yourself enough to succeed, improve, and grow in your mental and physical well-being. You need three new attitudes. The first is to choose yourself, the second is to give yourself, and the third is to transform stress. This reinvents your perceptions and builds an invaluable skill—emotional intelligence. It can be done by adopting the six-second model of emotional intelligence (EQ).

Six-Second Model of EQ

Emotional intelligence is more than a skill; it's a way of life, attitude, virtue, and an optimal mind-body mindset to achieve everything you need, including improved health, better living, and an adaptive mental state. EQ blends feelings and thoughts so you can perform optimally in your condition to improve your quality of life. It's also a key skill to better relationships with yourself and others, which is necessary for overall well-being. Intelligence isn't the only skill you possess to succeed at your goals; it also requires emotional intelligence. Daniel Goleman designed the famous six-second model of EQ in 1995 as an action plan to achieve a change of mindset that allows you to be flexible enough to make changes to your health and life (Freedman, 2010).

The action plan requires a commitment to being more aware of your mindset and knowing what you do when stress presents itself. It also requires intention so you do what you mean and purpose so you do it for a reason. You must know yourself, including what you do, feel, perceive, and think. Knowing yourself provides the 'what' of your mindset change. You'll know what your resources are, such as strengths, qualities, and available support. You'll also know what challenges you, what you desire, and what you want to change. To choose yourself is to do what you mean to do instead of running on autopilot when stress presents itself. Choosing yourself provides the 'how' so you can feel competent enough to actively respond. You'll know what actions are required, and how to influence others and yourself.

To give yourself is to do it so that purpose can drive your motivation and competency. Giving yourself provides the 'why' so you're clear on your goals and have the energy to pursue them. This helps you stay focused on why you must respond in a certain way. You'll know why you need to move in new directions and why you need people to support you. When it comes to health improvement, it's a lonely and long journey without social support. Think of this trio as a circle because it's a process and not a list. Your action plan can only work if you keep spinning the circle to use each concept. The circle spins faster as you move through these actions, and your momentum grows. Each of the trio requirements also needs one of eight competencies to work.

Knowing yourself requires you to enhance your emotional literacy and acknowledge patterns. You must pursue the knowledge and awareness of your mindset and perceptions. Understand the emotions that come from it, and know that your perceptions are flexible. Can you see patterns in your stress evaluation methods? To pursue emotional literacy, you must find the patterns that make it more difficult than it needs to be. Enhanced emotional literacy includes accurately identifying complex and simple emotions in yourself and others before you interpret them. Don't make assumptions, and don't allow yourself to jump on the train before you see the negative habits of evaluation. Recognize the frequency of your habits and how you behave and react to them.

Choosing yourself requires you to consider the consequences of thoughts, navigate emotions, and adopt intrinsic motivation and optimism. You'll find it difficult to take action without intrinsic motivation or positive thinking. You must look for opportunities in challenges. Pessimists can't see opportunities. They only see threats. Applying consequential thinking to choose yourself is as simple as weighing your pros and cons.

Interrogate yourself for a moment by asking whether the situation will harm you.

Perhaps, it might benefit you in the long-term. Seek the potential benefits, and recognize whether you have the resources you need to achieve the desired outcome. You must navigate your emotions to transform, harness, and assess your resources. Engage with your intrinsic motivation by assessing how the goal makes you feel. Are you pursuing health and mindset changes according to your personal values, or are they based on external expectations and conditioning? Finally, exercise optimism because it's the only way to adopt a proactive perspective that includes possibilities and hope.

Giving yourself requires you to adopt noble goals and increased empathy. You're already increasing your empathy if you respond to your emotions appropriately. Recognize and connect with your emotions to respond accurately. Only choose to pursue noble goals, too. Otherwise, your daily choices won't coincide with your purpose or values. Everyone has a purpose in this world, and it's the main component required for contentment, improved health, and positive mindsets. You can't think positively about something that goes against your purpose. Your purpose is possibly to improve your fitness levels so your heart condition interferes less with your daily life.

The purpose here is to improve cardiovascular health for a better quality of life and not your ability to lift more weights. Your health goals and mindset change must also align with your purposes outside of your current health conditions, which is done when you improve your fitness so you can enjoy your kids without heaving and breathlessness. Your purpose is to provide a good life for your children. It's not your only purpose, but it makes a difference to your health goals.

The three pursuits combined with the eight actions reconfigure your perception of your health and life. It also clarifies what needs to be done and gives you a method of achieving it. You can't imagine the changes your future holds for health and overall well-being once you change the way you see stress, challenges, and your ability to fulfill the resources required to meet the demand of stressful situations. You're nearly ready to change the way your health has declined, but you must first learn about the facts behind 'miraculous' recoveries.

Chapter 7:

The Problem of Miraculous Medical Recoveries

Miracle cures have been around for centuries, but the phenomenon is vastly misunderstood by most people. Science doesn't like the word 'miracle.' Science is about pinpointing the cause of such a phenomenon and the understanding of what causes the spontaneous medical recoveries have been documented for hundreds of years. You'll learn an incredible truth surrounding the puzzling recoveries and the science that explains the phenomenon. The cause and root of these 'miracles' are closely related to what you've already learned in this book. So, are there miracles in medicine? The scientific nature of medicine disputes the probability of it. There are some case studies where mainstream science couldn't explain what caused the recovery, but could this be a result of the mind-body connection?

The Spontaneous Regression and Remission of Cancer

Cancer in any form is one of the most devastating and life-threatening conditions that exist today. If a condition could be called a death sentence, cancer would be it. However, there have been some strange phenomena and recoveries tied to this horrific condition that dispute the idea of it being a death sentence. Case studies have been coming to light about patients who refuse treatment and survive. Not only do they survive, they also outlive cancer. They spend the rest of their lives as free as someone who has no malignant cancer cells. Indeed, everyone develops cancer cells throughout their lives, but only certain people develop cancer. Cancer has ripped apart lives and families for centuries, but some case studies have led to the evolution of understanding how some people defeated death. These people stared at the grim reaper and said "not today."

One of the most common oddities has been the spontaneous regression or remission of cancer. The word 'spontaneous' indicates a change that doesn't have an apparent cause. Cancer patients mostly hear the word progression with every ounce of fear that follows; however, regression is the opposite. It means the tumor has regressed partially or completely. In some cases, the tumor has disappeared from imaging devices. Intriguing, this phenomenon has been studied for eons to find answers to the devastating condition. Doctor Thomas Jessy from the Department of Oral Medicine and Radiology in Bangalore, India, reviewed the literature containing hundreds if not thousands of case studies and the history of how these 'miracles' were understood in medicine (Jessy, 2011). It started way before modern knowledge.

The history of this field of study delved deep into the reasons why tumors were disappearing without any medical treatment, surgery, or interventions that could cure cancer. Many cases were documented where patients did not receive adequate interventions to bring about the results they experienced. Indeed, spontaneous implies that there's no known cause, but Jessy's research exposed a few key factors in the phenomenon. The oldest record of this phenomenon was when Italian Saint Peregrine Laziozi, who died in 1345, presented with cancer of the tibia. The tumor was huge enough to break through his skin, and he required an amputation of his leg. His tumor became severely infected while it was exposed to external bacteria before the amputation.

To his physician's surprise, Peregrine's tumor was completely gone by the time he was supposed to undergo surgery. Not only did his tumor vanish, he also lived a full life without it returning. His story is the reason why spontaneously disappearing tumors are called Saint Peregrine's tumors. Today, the literature surrounding the miraculous dissipation of tumors is closely connected to infections, including diphtheria, smallpox, measles, malaria, influenza, and tuberculosis among others. Nonetheless, there was a strong connection between acute infections and spontaneous regression in cancer patients. Doctor William Coley was a young bone surgeon at New York Memorial Hospital when he started his search for better treatment after losing his first cancer patient. His first interest was a young immigrant who had an egg-sized sarcoma on his cheek.

The patient underwent surgery to remove the tumor on two occasions, but it would keep returning as a smaller sarcoma near his ear. The surgery left the young man with a wound that couldn't be repaired, even with a skin graft. Ironically, this open wound would become infected with Streptococcus-induced erysipelas, which is an acute bacterial infection, and the patient's tumor would disappear. The infection raged through him, causing a high fever, but once it broke, the patient began healing and continued to live without cancer. Coley realized the connection between the infection and the man's spontaneous cure. It lied in the immune response during the infection. Coley started experimenting on introducing infectious bacteria to tumors to turn the immune response on to the abnormal cells.

His first experiment didn't go too well. It wasn't easy to induce controlled infections with live bacteria in the nineteenth century. Sadly, a few experiments were fatal when the infection wasn't under control. However, a few experiments led to the answer he wanted. The infection caused a reaction in the body, switching the immune system on to attack tumors. The science behind vaccines was developing well, and Coley turned to this evolution to introduce bacteria to his patients. He injected them with either a Gram-positive Streptococcus pyogenes or a Gram-negative Serratia marcescens vaccine that contained dead bacteria, which was just enough to induce the desired infection. The immunotherapy developed by Coley was based on the vaccine called Coley's toxins.

According to research published in *The National Library of Medicine*, Coley's toxins are a highly effective method to induce fever, chills, and inflammation without the risk of losing control (Richardson et al., 1999). This quickly became immunotherapy that activated the immune system in patients whose immune systems weren't latching onto the abnormal cancer cells, even in patients with metastasis. Metastasis is when cancer spreads, but Coley's method was designed to trick the mind-body connection into creating a systemic immune response. Coley's daughter continued his legacy in the early 1900s by developing more vaccines that targeted specific immune responses, which dissipated sarcomas, melanomas, lymphomas, carcinomas, and myelomas.

Immunotherapy was an effective treatment option for various types of cancer, even in the terminal stages of it. Localized and systemic immunotherapy was the most effective, and it had to be an acute infection stimulated over a period of time. Patients were receiving daily or every other day shots to prevent resistance to the vaccines, and the dosage was gradually increased. The shots were also directly administered to the tumor or metastasis area if this was possible for the individual patient. Coley's work produced a safer way of introducing infections to cancer patients, which didn't only make them survive the average life expectancy, it also made them live cancer-free lives. The last recorded use of Coley's toxins in the historical review was in China in the 1980s.

A man was cured of liver cancer after receiving 68 injections over 34 weeks. Stimulated immunotherapy suffered a natural death in the latter half of the 1900s for numerous reasons. Surgery was becoming a sterile procedure, and postsurgical infections were fewer with the development of antibiotics intended to kill the same bacteria that could save lives. Surgery was always the first option for cancer patients, and scientific medicine didn't pay much attention to making people sick before curing them. Radiotherapy and chemotherapy were also gaining momentum, even though they suppressed the immune system. The worst reason lies in ethics. Surgeons administered antibiotics after surgery to prevent patient discomfort from fever.

Modern cancer treatments have flaws of their own. How can we turn the same system off that intends to preserve us? Turning the immune system off is partly the reason why traditional cancer treatments take so long, even if they work sometimes. Radiation and chemotherapy interfere with human cells, creating an inability to divide, which makes the immune system incapable of the cell division required in healing. Dendritic cells cannot release cytokines, explaining why traditional cancer therapies introduce synthetic cytokines to the body. Cytokines need to create inflammation to prevent abnormal cells from escaping the infected region, which is the cancerous tumor in this case. Cancer is not truly considered curable in scientific terms.

Patients enter remission or regression, but the disease often returns. Cancer is measured in probable survival rates, which used to be five years and has now been reduced to three years. When you're diagnosed, a doctor might tell you that the survival rate of your type and stage of cancer is two years. Not only must you undergo surgery or therapies that make you sick for long periods as opposed to short-lived acute infections, but this survival rate doesn't include your chances of being disease-free for life. The treatment options also come with a myriad of risks. *The Annals of Surgery* published a review of the risks involved with cancer surgery, looking at the positive and the negative (van der Bijl et al., 2009).

Keep in mind that surgical intervention even includes the biopsy that takes a sample of your tumor with a needle. Firstly, the wall surrounding the tumor is broken down during surgical intervention, making it easier for metastasis or the spread of cancer cells, and secondly, the cancer cells risk entering your bloodstream and traveling to various organs and tissue. Metastasis is a severe risk of fatality in cancer patients, and surgery can provoke it. Spontaneous regression and stimulated immunotherapy have broken the bonds this life-threatening condition holds over us, but is modern medicine undoing all the progress in curing cancer?

Sadly, traditional cancer treatment is also unable to identify between abnormal and normal cells in the body, tearing your health down further. Natural bacteria are automatically capable of stimulating the immune system so it can attack the abnormalities. Immunotherapy activates the dendritic cells to begin the body's self-healing process, but radiation and chemotherapy can deactivate these cells. However, certain cancer cells become invisible to the immune system, which makes modern intervention crucial to finding these cells before immunotherapy is applied. This allows a practitioner to target specific cells with bacteria that stimulate the innate immune response.

Systemic immunotherapy has higher success rates because the biological response is activated by a fever that allows cytotoxic cells to seek and destroy any abnormalities. Fever is one of the only biological states severe enough to recognize hidden cancer cells, and T cells are released to circulate through your system, looking for cancer agents to eradicate. The Bnai Zion Medical Center in Israel also concluded that the T cells and cytotoxins required to eliminate hidden cancer agents are stimulated by causing an inflammatory immune response (Tadmor, 2019). The immune system is the key, and this proves that there's science behind 'miracles.'

Miracles are events that occur once in a lifetime, but the body's self-healing ability is more common than most people think. *The Archives of Internal Medicine Journal* published a study that proved how common spontaneous regression is among patients of invasive breast cancer (Zahl et al., 2008). Using mammography to determine how often patients spontaneously regress from this disturbing and common cancer, researchers established that 22% of patients recovered without medical intervention. Breast cancer screening allows us to detect cancer even before men and women feel breast lumps, which indicates that we could expand this number in other cancer types if screening was more efficient.

The cause behind spontaneous regression is undoubtedly the immune system. It gives us the ability to fight cancer from the inside. Immunotherapy allows us to stimulate the immune system to combat cancer. These regressions were once called anomalies, but there's nothing exceptional about the body healing itself. Every cancer type and age is unique. Every cancer cell is as unique as a grain of sand on the beach because its molecular structure is different from any other type, including other cancer cells in your body. These cells might look similar under a microscope, but their molecular structure behaves uniquely from every other cell. The immune system is capable of learning the behavior of each cancer cell before eliminating it.

Doctor Louella Crawford was diagnosed with stage three breast cancer when she started researching quantum physics, spirituality, neuroscience, neuroplasticity, and psychoneuroimmunology to defeat the disease on her terms (Leukaemia Foundation, 2019). She stumbled on the effects of meditation and mindfulness because one thing she certainly knew was that the mind-body connection was the key to activating the immune system to kill cancer. Meditation slows your brain waves, changes the way your brain functions, and increases the depth of the grey matter. Our coherence is improved, and our mind-body connection functions better.

Moreover, meditation even increases T cells in the immune system, and this is the key to eradicating metastatic cancer. It's a free treatment option for sick individuals with many conditions beyond cancer. Additionally, it reduces stress, which coincides with Epel's telomere strands you learned about in the previous chapter. The ability to increase your telomere strands also reduces neuroticism or the excessive influx of anxiety and fear. Keep in mind that telomere strands are part of our genetic makeup, which means that meditation can also repair genetic flaws. Cancer malignancy is mainly genetic, so repairing the strands also reduces your risks for and from cancer. Mindfulness and meditation were Crawford's first lines of defense against her condition.

Crawford also delved into positive psychology. The mind has so much influence over physiological changes, so she knew that targeting a changed mindset, including her thoughts, beliefs, and emotional responses, could guide her condition to regression. Positive psychology teaches you to enhance certain virtues and skills, such as resilience, gratitude, compassion, forgiveness, positivity, and living in the present moment. Positive psychology is the pursuit of a wholehearted, good life that includes personal and social success. It also directs us to find our purpose in this life, and it includes not feeling alone in this big world. Cancer patients require support from their loved ones, and this can help them control their mind-body connection to achieve regression.

The most incredible realization Crawford reached was that our thoughts, emotions, and behaviors influence the way our genes express themselves. Changing your mindset, the way your brain functions, and your immune responses are the cornerstones of fighting cancer on the same playing field. Don't think of spontaneous regression as a miracle. It's something you're in full control of. Spontaneous regression of cancer is no longer a medical mystery or miracle. The Spontaneous Remission Bibliography Project collected data and evidence to support the disappearance or partial regression of cancer without medical interventions, which seemed unexplainable at first. The Noetic Institute of Science published the collection of literature under medical science, and it's called *Spontaneous Remission: An Annotated Bibliography*.

The Bredesen Protocol

Another medical mystery is coined the Bredesen Protocol, and it's also commonly mistaken for a miracle. Alzheimer's disease (AD) is a gut-wrenching, life-changing condition where your mind, memories, and cognitions decline. It's like watching yourself wither away like a plant that receives no nutrients and water. It's one of the hardest conditions for families to deal with, too. It's sad to watch someone who was once alive and jolly wither away slowly before your eyes until they don't know who you are or they can't remember how to speak. Alzheimer's is a degenerative disorder, which declines cognitive abilities, and it might even present as a shrinkage of the brain. Some stories of regeneration have made their rounds, but the advancement of the treatment for AD doesn't come from traditional medicine.

Doctor Dale Bredesen is an expert in neurodegenerative disorders at the Duke University Medical Center in Durham, North Carolina, and he has stumbled on how Alzheimer's can be reversed in the early stages of the disease (Transcendental Meditation, 2017). Bredesen understood that Alzheimer's wasn't a single disease. It had everything to do with the mind-body connection. Traditional medicine was focusing on managing Alzheimer's as a single-factor disease, affecting one part of the body. Their focus is solely based on the brain where cognitive decline occurs. They don't broaden their view to see all the holes in the story. Even science agrees that the brain is connected to every function in the body and mind, so why would you only target neurological repair and skip the root causes of it?

Think of the disease as a roof over your head. Different holes start forming in this roof, and rain starts pouring through. Present-day treatments from modern medicine give you plugs to stop the big holes that represent cognitive decline. What happens to the smaller holes forming across your roof? They spread, causing bigger holes and leaks again. If cognitive decline was a big hole and other lifestyle and health issues were smaller holes, the small holes always lead to bigger holes when you leave them unattended. Cognitive degeneration happens because of three root causes. Type one Alzheimer's is also called the hot root, and it's caused by chronic inflammation. Undiagnosed chronic inflammatory conditions can lead to cognitive decline, and so can your lifestyle choices if they promote inflammation.

Type two Alzheimer's is also called the cold root, and it's caused by nutritional deficiency when you eat the wrong foods throughout your life. This is an interesting type of decline because it has nothing to do with the brain per se, but what you eat can degenerate the brain. Type three Alzheimer's is also called the vile root, and it's caused by toxicity in the body and brain. Overexposure to mercury, copper, biotoxins, gluten, and other toxins found in food modern products lead to type three Alzheimer's. Bredesen developed the Bredesen Protocol to target treatment for every hole so the body can heal, which in turn, heals the brain. His research and treatment program allowed one of his patients to live five years beyond her initial decline without succumbing to it.

Bredesen knew that the brain, sleeping patterns, hormone levels, nutrients, gut health, metabolism, stress, cognitive stimulation, and a healthier immune system can change the decline, even reversing it in some patients. The gut is made of billions of bacteria called the microbiome, and they aren't all bad guys. Take someone with type two Alzheimer's. Their decline was activated by nutritional deficiency, which eventually declined their cognitions. The bacteria in your gut are responsible for collecting nutrients from food and removing toxins, and the failure to do so can starve the brain of what it needs for optimal functions. The bacteria can also be harmed by toxic foods, which leads to type three Alzheimer's.

Your body can't metabolize glucose for energy in the neural networks anymore, and the toxins cause inflammation in various brain regions to stop the functions from activating. Alzheimer's is developed through lifestyles that change the metabolism in your body, making it difficult for the brain to function as it should. Trans fats and refined sugars are part of the problem because the body metabolizes these for energy instead of turning on fat cells to create ketosis. Stress is another major factor that declines the brain, especially in the hippocampus region.

Stress tears down your cognitive network with endless bouts of cortisol, but it also breaks the walls in your stomach, leading to a leaky gut syndrome, which also promotes cognitive decline. The bacteria that must remove toxins break into fragments that flood your bloodstream, and these toxins make their way to the brain. This can also cause chronic inflammation in the brain because toxins are unwelcome disturbances, and inflammatory Alzheimer's leads to the development of type one. Even though there are three types of Alzheimer's, there's a delicate connection between them. The latest study conducted by Bredesen and his colleagues managed to reverse the cognitive decline in 100 patients with early symptoms and impairment (Bredesen et al., 2018).

Cognitive decline wasn't the only thing reversed in the study. Patients once restricted were able to return to work again. Bredesen's protocol is to target every aspect of degenerative conditions, including their fallout, such as dementia. Transcendental meditation is one method of reversing the effects or preventing the decline. It allows us to regain focus and control while it lowers blood pressure, stress, and inflammation caused by excessive cortisol. Transcendental meditation can reset the hormonal balance you require, and it sharpens the mind while you're repairing the damage. The functionality of the brain doesn't stop during Alzheimer's; it's the functioning that stops. Cognitive stimulation through neuroplasticity or neurogenesis activates these regions again.

Treatment includes a change in dietary habits, exercises, and mental stimulation. The protocol covers 36 metabolic factors that influence the decline, and it focuses on replacing nutrients and vitamins that promote a reboot in the diseased part of the brain. This model of treating and reversing Alzheimer's isn't a miracle. It merely requires you to practice meditation, mindfulness, physical activity, and dietary changes. The keto diet is a good option to keep your gut healthy while you practice your focus and keep your brain functioning well enough to maintain a healthy metabolism. It doesn't include the toxins, and it replaces them with health-promoting ingredients. There are no miracles when it comes to your health. It's up to you how healthy and long you live.

Bob Cafaro's Incredible Recovery

Bob Cafaro's journey has often been called a miracle, but it's not quite miraculous (Friedman, 2016). Cafaro was always intrigued by music, and he worked hard to master his cello at a young age. He was born on Long Island and knew his destiny at the age of 16. He visited the Saratoga Performing Arts Center (SPAC) in his junior year, and he sat at the back when he realized that classical music was his calling. He listened to the orchestra play a composition by Italian-American Composer John Carlo Mennoti when he could feel the music travel through him. His newly amplified passion got him into the Juilliard School of Arts in 1976, and he promised himself that he'd play at SPAC soon enough. Cafaro became a cellist for the Philadelphia Orchestra that frequented SPAC, and his purpose was fulfilled.

He was determined, talented, and incredibly masterful of the art of orchestral music, and he loved playing Ludwig van Beethoven's compositions. He looked up to Beethoven's legacy because the man went deaf before he composed his masterpieces. How can someone compose such greatness with no ability to hear? Nevertheless, it was early 1999 when Cafaro suffered his first multiple sclerosis (MS) attack. His leg went numb, and he lost control, tripping over the stage. Two months later, Cafaro suffered his second attack, which affected his peripheral vision in one eye. He was examined by a neurologist who also completed numerous scans to confirm that Cafaro had MS. Cafaro was a determined 40-year-old man who knew the risks of MS, which is an autoimmune disorder that makes the immune system attack the protective coating around nerve cells in the spine and brain.

It's both an autoimmune and degenerative disorder, and it has a poor prognosis due to its complexity. Cafaro went another four months before his third attack. He assumed it was a stomach bug because he couldn't keep his food and liquids down. He also had a sense of vertigo, which is a loss of balance. Cafaro ended up in the hospital after a week of severe dehydration, and he lost the use of his hands four days after his release. He couldn't play the cello at that point. Cafaro returned to his neuro-ophthalmologist who conducted a simple eye exam, but he was unable to read even the largest letters. He went on to fail the click test to determine whether he could see flashes, too. Doctor Robert Sergott only had one solution for Cafaro after realizing how much damage the autoimmune disorder was causing.

He told Cafaro that he'd give him a letter to confirm permanent disability. Utterly enraged, Cafaro refused to accept this traumatic news. He even got a little wordy with his doctor and promised him that he'll be back at work when the new season started six weeks later. Sergott doubted this, but Cafaro wasn't the kind of man who gave up. He threw himself into the research behind autoimmune disorders, and he quickly realized that there was one common link. The mind-connection was at the heart of the disease, and so was the cure. Cafaro received the news in 1999, and he denied the power to his diagnosis. He learned about the placebo and nocebo theories, and this explained how his condition worsened with medical negativity. He wasn't part of some statistic, and he'll prove it by adopting the placebo effect.

Cafaro started improving his condition by practicing meditation twice daily for 30 minutes. Meditation allows us to activate the placebo effect by creatively visualizing ourselves in better conditions. Cafaro visualized himself as healthy and capable of playing his cello so he could trick the brain into repairing the damaged nerve coatings. Neuroplasticity and neurogenesis allowed him to heal the scars and lesions on his brain. He also adopted the "water cure" to drink half his body weight in ounces of water daily. Cafaro believes that this provided his body with nutrients and hydration, which keeps the mind and body connection functioning at its best. Please note that the water cure is only advised under medical supervision. You can't simply start drinking half your body weight in water. Speak to your physician about it first.

Anyway, it was on a visit to Shenandoah National Park in Virginia where Cafaro spent time in nature to meditate and remain in the present moment that he reached a new epiphany. Cafaro came across a deer sign urging park visitors not to feed the deer because human food can take 30% of their lifespan away. A lightbulb lit up, and Cafaro knew he had to remove everything he found harmful through his research. This included anything non-organic, unethically raised, processed, refined, saturated, and toxic. Gluten was removed from his diet, and so was chocolate, meat, and dairy products. He changed his diet to leafy green, organic vegetables and natural foods only. He includes a lot of raw nuts, cold-pressed olive oil, sunflower seeds, and foods that contain antioxidants and anti-inflammatory agents to combat his disease.

Not only did Cafaro return to work six weeks later, but he also gradually improved his health by adding mindfulness, meditation, clean eating, and bicycling to his daily routine. He was fortunate to meet another name synonymous with defying the odds in 2013. Nando Parrado and Cafaro had one thing in common. They both shouldn't be alive today.

Parrado was one of the survivors of the 1972 plane crash in the Andes mountain range, and he was left for dead between the cold bodies when survivors realized that his skull was fractured in multiple places. However, he woke up 72 hours later, and with his mind over matter attitude, he walked for 72 days through the wintery mountain range until he found help.

Cafaro and Parrado both believe they shouldn't have survived their ordeals, and truthfully, most people wouldn't. Cafaro then decided to pay neuro-ophthalmologist Sergott another visit in 2013 to examine his progress on brain scans. The scans confirmed that Cafaro had no lesions on his brain, even though he originally had 50. Sergott was amazed at Cafaro's ability to heal himself through simple daily practices and lifestyle changes. Cafaro doesn't consider his recovery to be miraculous. He considers it evidence that we can control our health and recovery from any disease as long as we focus on a healthy mind-body connection. From placebos to simple dietary changes, Cafaro defied the odds.

It's not necessary to understand the neurological, psychological, and physical changes Cafaro experienced because you've already learned how to adopt each of these changes in your mind-body connection. Moreover, it's been proven through science that you can have faith in your healing from the inside. Miracles might exist, but none of the stories covered in this chapter describe miracles. They describe people who used the power of mind of matter to guarantee that the mind-body connection can do what it was intended to do—heal itself. Never underestimate the power of healing thought again.

Conclusion

Thoughts and emotions are a window into a healthier mind and body. Their healing properties can help you navigate the most dangerous chronic conditions and allow you the freedom to live on your terms again. Poor health takes no prisoners, and it plays no favorites. People in the prime of their lives are stricken with chronic conditions.

You think that your thirties is where it all happens. You build a career, start a family, have a bustling social life, and you're about to buy a house. This is what it looks like in the movies with white picket fences. What the movies don't show is that this prime stage of your development and foundation in life is often fraught with poor health.

Being young can make us feel invincible. There's always tomorrow when it comes to better living. Maybe you've already been practicing some healthier options, but you're still unwell. How can someone this young be diagnosed with diabetes? Where does the autoimmune disorder come from, and how can your heart not be in peak shape?

In comes the forties, and you're still battling with conditions that shouldn't be part of your life. Since when do young people get sick? You're aiming for the top position at work. Heck, you might even be aiming to be the boss. The only bad thing in your life is that your health isn't what it should be at this wonderful age.

Then, we have a person who gets diagnosed with cancer. Life doesn't seem so linear anymore. The picket fence movies got it all wrong. It doesn't matter what your doctor diagnoses you with; what matters is that your life has restricting chains placed over it. To make it worse, your mental health is on a downward trajectory now.

Understandably, we all wish to be the poster children for healthy living. Sometimes, we focus on improving our health before it all goes wrong. Maybe you don't have a chronic condition, but you fear the potential inheritance of degenerative disorders in your golden years. Either way, placing a priceless value over your health is the best thing you can do.

Moreover, it doesn't require rigorous changes to your life. The mind-body connection is all you need, and your thoughts and emotions will guide it to prime health. The connection between your body and mind is much clearer now. Who knew that emotions were physical? Understanding the differences in the terminology used also helps.

The brain and mind are distinct in meaning. Health is also another misunderstood concept to many. It's about more than your ability to run marathons or climb stairs without heaving. It even contains social factors. Your new understanding of health also helps you see why psychoneuroimmunology is the key to exceptional well-being.

The immune system is such a delicate part of your being, and your emotions and thoughts are heavily involved in its functions. Stress is the main obstacle that stands between you and perfect health. It tears down your neural network, and it causes chaos throughout your body. Neuroplasticity is the answer, and knowing how to use it improves your chances.

Moreover, you know the difference between neuroplasticity and neurogenesis. The brain is capable of incredible feats, including self-healing. You simply need to reinvent the brain, and sometimes, it's as simple as smiling. You also know how to turn the PNS on so you can activate the relaxation response with numerous, proven strategies.

Meditation, yoga, and visualization are only a few of the relaxing techniques you can use. A relaxed mind-body connection is a smart mind-body connection. Learning about the placebo and nocebo effects also protects you from the biological influence of an unwanted diagnosis, and they can be used to improve your health instead.

A theory about perceptions has changed your outlook, making your health and life a lot simpler. You can turn your negative health influences into something incredible, and when everything else fails, use the proven science behind so-called miracles to inspire yourself. A vital change is required in your thoughts, and then you can live on your terms.

My research and travels opened the possibility of optimal health, inside and outside. Years later, I'm still the poster child for health, and I didn't need to sacrifice anything to get here. My wish is for you to reach my state, and I trust you will. Social aspects are a huge part of better health, so feel free to leave an honest review to help others.

A final piece of advice is that you prioritize your health because you only live once. Everything you do, feel, and think is paving your legacy. Make sure it's paved with positive, healthy, and happy experiences.

References

Ackerman, C. (2018, July 25). *What is neuroplasticity? A psychologist explains [+14 exercises]*. Positive Psychology. https://positivepsychology.com/neuroplasticity/

Alegre, A. A., & Zumaeta, P. A. (2015). Relationship between mind and brain: A proposal of solution based on forms of intra- and extra-individual negentropy. *Propósitos y Representaciones*, 3(1), 289–311. https://doi.org/10.20511/pyr2015.v3n1.73

Apollo Health. (n.d.). *The end of Alzheimer's*. Apollo Health. https://www.apollohealthco.com/book/the-end-of-alzheimers/

Bender, J. (2013, December 9). *What are the differences between PTS and PTSD?* BrainLine. https://www.brainline.org/article/what-are-differences-between-pts-and-ptsd

Berecz, J. (1976). *Towards a monastic philosophy of man*. In Andrews Education (pp. 279–288). https://www.andrews.edu/library/car/cardigital/Periodicals/AUSS/1976-2/1976-2-02.pdf

Bergland, C. (2017, February 6). *How do neuroplasticity and neurogenesis rewire your brain?* Psychology Today. https://www.psychologytoday.com/za/blog/the-athletes-way/201702/how-do-neuroplasticity-and-neurogenesis-rewire-your-brain

Biancolli, A. (2016, August 10). *Philadelphia orchestra cellist beats MS*. Times Union. https://www.timesunion.com/local/article/Philadelphia-Orchestra-cellist-beats-MS-9133564.php

Bredesen, D., Sharlin, K., Jenkins, D., Okuno, M., Youngberg, W., Cohen, S. H., Stefani, A., Brown, R. L., Conger, S., Tanio, C., Hathaway, A., Cogan, M., Hagedorn, D., Amos, E., Amos, A., Bergman, N., Diamond, C., Lawrence, J., Rusk, I. M., ... Braud, M. (2018, November 5). *Reversal of cognitive decline: 100 patients*. David Perlmutter M.D. https://www.drperlmutter.com/study/reversal-of-cognitive-decline-100-patients/

Byjus Learning App. (2020). *Important difference between brain and mind*. BYJUS. https://byjus.com/biology/difference-between-brain-and-mind/

Calcia, M. A., Bonsall, D. R., Bloomfield, P. S., Selvaraj, S., Barichello, T., & Howes, O. D. (2016). Stress and neuroinflammation: A systematic review of the effects of stress on microglia and the implications for mental illness. *Psychopharmacology*, 233(9), 1637–1650. https://doi.org/10.1007/s00213-016-4218-9

Catholic Charities. (n.d.). *Managing stress more effectively the relaxation response*. Catholic Charities. http://catholiccharitiesla.org/wp-content/uploads/Managing-Stress-The-Relaxation-Response-TS-2-04.pdf

Cherry, K. (2011, April 16). *How the placebo effect works in psychology*. Verywell Mind. https://www.verywellmind.com/what-is-the-placebo-effect-2795466

Clark, D. A., & Beck, A. T. (2010). Cognitive theory and therapy of anxiety and depression: Convergence with neurobiological findings. *Trends in Cognitive Sciences*, 14(9), 418–424. https://doi.org/10.1016/j.tics.2010.06.007

Cognifit Research. (n.d.). *Relationship of the brain and the mind*. Cognifit Research. https://www.cognifit.com/mind

Conyers, J. (2018, May 30). *The effects of stress and how yoga can help*. Jill Conyers. https://jillconyers.com/2018/05/yoga-helps-stress-symptoms/

Deak, T., Quinn, M., Cidlowski, J. A., Victoria, N. C., Murphy, A. Z., & Sheridan, J. F. (2015). Neuroimmune mechanisms of stress: Sex differences, developmental plasticity, and implications for pharmacotherapy of stress-related disease. *Stress (Amsterdam, Netherlands)*, 18(4), 367–380. https://doi.org/10.3109/10253890.2015.1053451

Demarin, V., & Morović, S. (2014). Neuroplasticity. *Periodicum Biologorum*, 116(2), 209–211. https://hrcak.srce.hr/126369

Eldridge, L., & Jelic, S. (2020, January 19). *How common is spontaneous remission of cancer?* Verywell Health. https://www.verywellhealth.com/spontaneous-remission-of-lung-cancer-a-rare-miracle-3971875

Epel, E. S., Blackburn, E. H., Lin, J., Dhabhar, F. S., Adler, N. E., Morrow, J. D., & Cawthon, R. M. (2004). Accelerated telomere shortening in response to life stress. *Proceedings of the National Academy of Sciences*, 101(49), 17312–17315. https://doi.org/10.1073/pnas.0407162101

Freedman, J. (2010, January 28). *The six seconds model of emotional intelligence: EQ in action*. Six Seconds. https://www.6seconds.org/2010/01/27/the-six-seconds-eq-model/

Freedman, P. (2019, April 16). *Threat or challenge? The surprising new science of how we think about stress • six seconds*. Six Seconds. https://www.6seconds.org/2019/04/16/threat-or-challenge-the-surprising-new-science-of-how-we-think-about-stress/

Friedman, S. (2016, February 5). *Haddon township cellist beats the odds over MS*. Courier-Post. https://www.courierpostonline.com/story/life/2016/02/05/haddon-township-cellist-multiple-sclerosis/79881466/

Fry, W. F., & Rader, C. (1977). The respiratory components of mirthful laughter. *Journal of Biological Psychology*, 19, 39–50. https://www.researchgate.net/publication/232517796_The_respiratory_components_of_mirthful_laughter/citation/download

Hampton, D. (2019, January 13). *How to heal the brain with neuroplasticity after injury.* The Best Brain Possible. https://thebestbrainpossible.com/healing-brain-neuroplasticity-trauma-injury/

Harvard Health Publishing. (2009, May). *Yoga for anxiety and depression.* Harvard Health. https://www.health.harvard.edu/mind-and-mood/yoga-for-anxiety-and-depression

Harvard Health Publishing. (2014, March). *The nocebo response.* Harvard Health. https://www.health.harvard.edu/newsletter_article/The_nocebo_response

Harvard Health Publishing. (2014, July 16). *What meditation can do for your mind, mood, and health.* Harvard Health. https://www.health.harvard.edu/staying-healthy/what-meditation-can-do-for-your-mind-mood-and-health-

Harvard Health Publishing. (2017, May 1). *The power of the placebo effect.* Harvard Health. https://www.health.harvard.edu/mental-health/the-power-of-the-placebo-effect

Harvard Health Publishing. (2018, May 1). *Understanding the stress response*. Harvard Health. https://www.health.harvard.edu/staying-healthy/understanding-the-stress-response

Harvey, S. (2017, May 29). *The science of the relaxation response*. Medibank Live Better. https://www.medibank.com.au/livebetter/be-magazine/wellbeing/the-science-of-the-relaxation-response/

Ho, R. C. M., Neo, L. F., Chua, A. N. C., Cheak, A. A. C., & Mak, A. (2010). Research on Psychoneuroimmunology: Does stress influence immunity and cause coronary artery disease? *Annals Academy of Medicine*, 39(3), 191–196. https://www.annals.edu.sg/pdf/39VolNo3Mar2010/V39N3p191.pdf

Hoenemeyer, T. W., Kaptchuk, T. J., Mehta, T. S., & Fontaine, K. R. (2018). Open-Label placebo treatment for cancer-related fatigue: A randomized-controlled clinical trial. *Scientific Reports*, 8(1). https://doi.org/10.1038/s41598-018-20993-y

Irwin, M. R., Olmstead, R., & Carroll, J. E. (2016). Sleep disturbance, sleep duration, and inflammation: A systematic review and meta-analysis of cohort studies and experimental sleep deprivation. *Biological Psychiatry*, 80(1), 40–52. https://doi.org/10.1016/j.biopsych.2015.05.014

Jamieson, J. P., Nock, M. K., & Mendes, W. B. (2012). Mind over matter: Reappraising arousal improves cardiovascular and cognitive responses to stress. *Journal of Experimental Psychology: General*, 141(3), 417–422. https://doi.org/10.1037/a0025719

Jessy, T. (2011). Immunity over inability: The spontaneous regression of cancer. *Journal of Natural Science, Biology, and Medicine*, 2(1), 43–49. https://doi.org/10.4103/0976-9668.82318

Kam-Hansen, S., Jakubowski, M., Kelley, J. M., Kirsch, I., Hoaglin, D. C., Kaptchuk, T. J., & Burstein, R. (2014). Altered placebo and drug labeling changes the outcome of episodic migraine attacks. *Science Translational Medicine*, 6(218), 218ra5-218ra5. https://doi.org/10.1126/scitranslmed.3006175

Kolb, B., Mychasiuk, R., Muhammad, A., & Gibb, R. (2013). Brain plasticity in the developing brain. *Changing Brains - Applying Brain Plasticity to Advance and Recover Human Ability*, 35–64. https://doi.org/10.1016/b978-0-444-63327-9.00005-9

Lazar, S. (2018, June 20). *Mindfulness meditation and relaxation response affect brain differently*. Harvard Gazette. https://news.harvard.edu/gazette/story/2018/06/mindfulness-meditation-and-relaxation-response-affect-brain-differently/

Leitan, N. D., & Murray, G. (2014). The mind-body relationship in psychotherapy: grounded cognition as an explanatory framework. *Frontiers in Psychology*, 5. https://doi.org/10.3389/fpsyg.2014.00472

Leukaemia Foundation. (2019, August 27). *The mind/body connection in healing*. Leukaemia Foundation. https://www.leukaemia.org.au/stories/mind-body-connection/

Lino, C. (2019, July 3). *Broaden-and-Build theory of positive emotions (+PDF)*. Positive Psychology. https://positivepsychology.com/broaden-build-theory/

Littrell, J. (2008). PDF the mind-body connection: Not just a theory anymore. *ResearchGate*, 46(4), 17–37. https://www.researchgate.net/publication/5263188_The_mind-body_connection_not_just_a_theory_anymore

Lumen Learning. (2012). *Psychoneuroimmunology and stress | disease prevention and healthy lifestyles*. Lumen Learning. https://courses.lumenlearning.com/diseaseprevention/chapter/psychoneuroimmunology-and-stress/

Marshall, G. D. (2011). The adverse effects of psychological stress on immunoregulatory balance: Applications to human inflammatory diseases. *Immunology and Allergy Clinics of North*

America, 31(1), 133–140. https://doi.org/10.1016/j.iac.2010.09.013

Martin, S. (2008). *The power of the relaxation response*. APA. https://www.apa.org/monitor/2008/10/relaxation

McDonald, P. G., O'Connell, M., & Lutgendorf, S. K. (2013). Psychoneuroimmunology and cancer: A decade of discovery, paradigm shifts, and methodological innovations. *Brain, Behavior, and Immunity*, 30, S1–S9. https://doi.org/10.1016/j.bbi.2013.01.003

Minded Institute. (n.d.). *Yoga for trauma: A holistic treatment pathway for PTSD*. The Minded Institute. https://themindedinstitute.com/yoga-trauma-and-ptsd/

Mitchell, M. (2013, March 29). *Dr. Herbert Benson's relaxation response*. Psychology Today. https://www.psychologytoday.com/us/blog/heart-and-soul-healing/201303/dr-herbert-benson-s-relaxation-response

Mondaini, N., Gontero, P., Giubilei, G., Lombardi, G., Cai, T., Gavazzi, A., & Bartoletti, R. (2007). Finasteride 5 mg and sexual side effects: How many of these are related to a nocebo phenomenon? *The Journal of Sexual Medicine*, 4(6), 1708–1712. https://doi.org/10.1111/j.1743-6109.2007.00563.x

Morris, A. (2013, July 8). *Stress appraisal: Challenge vs threat*. Believe Perform.

https://believeperform.com/stress-appraisal-challenge-vs-threat/

Mutter, P. (2018, December 21). *Science proves it - Alzheimer's can be prevented and reversed!* David Perlmutter M.D. https://www.drperlmutter.com/yes-alzheimers-can-be-reversed/

Newman, T. (2016, February 3). *Psychoneuroimmunology: Laugh and be well.* Medical News Today. https://www.medicalnewstoday.com/articles/305921#Different-stress

Pandya, S. (2011). Understanding brain, mind and soul: Contributions from neurology and neurosurgery. *Mens Sana Monographs*, 9(1), 129. https://doi.org/10.4103/0973-1229.77431

Pangambam, S. (2020, May 19). *The psychology of beating an incurable illness: Bob Cafaro (transcript).* The Singju Post. https://singjupost.com/the-psychology-of-beating-an-incurable-illness-bob-cafaro-transcript/

Pecina, M., Bohnert, A. S. B., Sikora, M., Avery, E. T., Langenecker, S. A., Mickey, B. J., & Zubieta, J.-K. (2015). Association between placebo-activated neural systems and antidepressant responses: Neurochemistry of placebo effects in major depression. *JAMA Psychiatry*, 72(11), 1087–1094. https://doi.org/10.1001/jamapsychiatry.2015.1335

Pfingsten, M., Leibing, E., Harter, W., Kröner-Herwig, B., Hempel, D., Kronshage, U., & Hildebrandt, J. (2001). Fear-Avoidance behavior and anticipation of pain in patients with chronic low back pain: A randomized controlled study. *Pain Medicine*, 2(4), 259–266. https://doi.org/10.1046/j.1526-4637.2001.01044.x

Physiopedia. (n.d.). Neuroplasticity. Physiopedia. https://www.physio-pedia.com/Neuroplasticity

Pikorn, I. (2019, September 18). *How to engage the relaxation response for stress-regulation.* Insight Timer Blog. https://insighttimer.com/blog/relaxation-response/

Poulin, M. J., & Holman, E. A. (2013). Helping hands, healthy body? Oxytocin receptor gene and prosocial behavior interact to buffer the association between stress and physical health. *Hormones and Behavior*, 63(3), 510–517. https://doi.org/10.1016/j.yhbeh.2013.01.004

Ramirez, D. (2020, September 16). *Exploring the mind-body connection through research.* Positive Psychology. https://positivepsychology.com/mind-body-connection/

Raypole, C. (2019, February 25). *Nocebo effect: When negative thinking impacts health.* Healthline. https://www.healthline.com/health/nocebo-effect#how-it-works

Reeves, R. R., Ladner, M. E., Hart, R. H., & Burke, R. S. (2007). Nocebo effects with antidepressant clinical drug trial placebos. *General Hospital Psychiatry*, 29(3), 275–277. https://doi.org/10.1016/j.genhosppsych.2007.01.010

Richardson, M. A., Ramirez, T., Russell, N. C., & Moye, L. A. (1999). Coley toxins immunotherapy: A retrospective review. *Alternative Therapies in Health and Medicine*, 5(3), 42–47. https://pubmed.ncbi.nlm.nih.gov/10234867/

Robinson, L. (2019, May 2). *Relaxation techniques for stress relief*. Help Guide. https://www.helpguide.org/articles/stress/relaxation-techniques-for-stress-relief.htm

Rosenfeld, J. (2018, April 11). *11 scientific benefits of having a laugh*. Mental Floss. https://www.mentalfloss.com/article/539632/scientific-benefits-having-laugh

Sahakian, B. J., Langley, C., & Kaser, M. (2020, May 11). *How chronic stress changes the brain – and what you can do to reverse the damage*. The Conversation. https://theconversation.com/how-chronic-stress-changes-the-brain-and-what-you-can-do-to-reverse-the-damage-133194

Saling, J. (2012, January 31). *What is the placebo effect?* WebMD. https://www.webmd.com/pain-management/what-is-the-placebo-effect#1

Science Direct. (n.d.). *Psychoneuroimmunology - an overview.* Science Direct. https://www.sciencedirect.com/topics/medicine-and-dentistry/psychoneuroimmunology

Scott, E. (2006, January 31). *The health benefits of laughter.* Verywell Mind. https://www.verywellmind.com/the-stress-management-and-health-benefits-of-laughter-3145084

Scott, E., & Goldman, R. (2019). *How to trigger your relaxation response.* Verywell Mind. https://www.verywellmind.com/what-is-the-relaxation-response-3145145

Scott, E., & Susman, D. (2019). *How is stress affecting my health?* Verywell Mind. https://www.verywellmind.com/stress-and-health-3145086

Seery, M. D. (2013). The biopsychosocial model of challenge and threat: Using the heart to measure the mind. *Social and Personality Psychology Compass*, 7(9), 637–653. https://doi.org/10.1111/spc3.12052

Seladi-Schulman, J. (2020, February 13). *Placebo effect: What it is, examples, and more.* Healthline. https://www.healthline.com/health/placebo-effect#the-psychology

Seladi-Schulman, J., & Falck, S. (2018, January 26). *Psychoneuroimmunology: Definition, research, and examples.* Healthline.

https://www.healthline.com/health/psychoneuroimmunology#takeaway

Skerrett, P. J. (2010, November 24). *Laugh and be thankful—it's good for the heart*. Harvard Health Blog. https://www.health.harvard.edu/blog/laugh-and-be-thankful-its-good-for-the-heart-20101124839

Slavich, G. M. (2019). Psychoneuroimmunology of stress and mental health. *The Oxford Handbook of Stress and Mental Health*, 518–546. https://doi.org/10.1093/oxfordhb/9780190681777.013.24

Stromberg, J. (2012, July 23). *What is the nocebo effect?* Smithsonian Magazine. https://www.smithsonianmag.com/science-nature/what-is-the-nocebo-effect-5451823/

Su, Y. S., Veeravagu, A., & Grant, G. (2016). Neuroplasticity after traumatic brain injury. *Translational Research in Traumatic Brain Injury*. https://pubmed.ncbi.nlm.nih.gov/26583189/

Tadmor, T. (2019). Time to understand more about spontaneous regression of cancer. *Acta Haematologica*, 141(3), 156–157. https://doi.org/10.1159/000496680

The Mind-Body Connection. (2010). *The mind-body connection*. Sage Hub (pp. 1–21). Hamilton. https://us.sagepub.com/sites/default/files/upm-assets/36857_book_item_36857.pdf

Transcendental Meditation. (2017, October 20). *Curing early-onset Alzheimer's: New research offers a ray of hope.* Transcendental Meditation. https://tmhome.com/benefits/curing-early-onset-alzheimers-research-bredesen-protocol-meditation/

Van der Bij, G. J., Oosterling, S. J., Beelen, R. H. J., Meijer, S., Coffey, J. C., & van Egmond, M. (2009). The perioperative period is an underutilized window of therapeutic opportunity in patients with colorectal cancer. *Annals of Surgery*, 249(5), 727–734. https://doi.org/10.1097/sla.0b013e3181a3ddbd

Wahbeh, H. (n.d.). *Spontaneous remission bibliography project.* IONS. https://noetic.org/research/spontaneous-remission-bibliography-project/

Warren, S. (2019, December 4). *The critical difference between challenge and threat stress responses.* Somatic Movement Center. https://somaticmovementcenter.com/challenge-threat-stress-response/

Watts, M. (2017, July 16). *How yoga reduces stress.* Just Mind. https://justmind.org/yoga-reduces-stress/

Well for Health. (n.d.). *What makes the bredesen protocol so effective in treating dementia?* The Well for Health. https://www.thewellforhealth.com/blog/what-makes-the-bredesen-protocol-so-effective-in-treating-dementia

Zahl, P. H., Maehlen, J., & Welch, H. G. (2008). The natural history of invasive breast cancers detected by screening mammography. *Archives of Internal Medicine*, 168(21), 2311–2316. https://doi.org/10.1001/archinte.168.21.2311

www.ingramcontent.com/pod-product-compliance
Lightning Source LLC
Chambersburg PA
CBHW020256030426
42336CB00010B/794